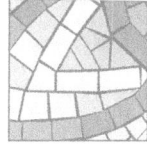

FACING ISLAM

WITHOUT FEAR:

A Christian's Guide to
Engaging the Muslim World

Also by Patrick Nachtigall...

Passport of Faith (Warner Press: 2006)

Faith in the Future (Warner Press: 2008)

Mosaic (Warner Press: 2010)

In God We Trust? (Warner Press: 2015)

FACING ISLAM
WITHOUT
FEAR:

A Christian's Guide to
Engaging the Muslim World

PATRICK NACHTIGALL

Published by Warner Press Inc.
Warner Press and the "WP" logo are trademarks of Warner Press Inc.

Copyright © 2015 by Patrick Nachtigall. All rights reserved.
Cover art and layout copyright © 2015 by Warner Press Inc.
Editors: A. Liverett
Cover Design: Curtis Corzine
Book Design: Karen Muilenburg

Warner Press, Inc.
PO Box 2499
Anderson, IN 46018-2499
800-741-7721
www.warnerpress.org

ISBN: 978-1-59317-794-2

Library of Congress Cataloging-in-Publication Data

Nachtigall, Patrick, 1970-
    Facing Islam without fear : a Christian's guide to engaging the Muslim world / by Patrick Nachtigall.
        pages cm
    Includes bibliographical references and index.
    ISBN 978-1-59317-794-2 (pbk. : alk. paper) -- ISBN 978-1-59317-801-7 (ebook : alk. paper)
    1. Islam. 2. Missions to Muslims. 3. Islam--Relations--Christianity. 4. Christianity and other religions--Islam. I. Title.
    BV2625.N33 2015
    261.2'7--dc23
                                            2015016438

Printed in the United States of America.

This book is dedicated to my dear father, Harry Nachtigall (1937–2013), who taught me to engage cultures and always look underneath the surface.

Table of Contents

Introduction

The life of a cross-cultural missionary is stressful. On the Holmes-Rahe stress scale, the average person scores one hundred. Anyone scoring over three hundred is probably having their body break down as the stress brings on physical illness. The average missionary scores six hundred, and that number goes as high as eight hundred to one thousand in the first year on the mission field. In my fourteen years on the mission field, my health has declined significantly, I have found myself in the hospital frequently, and truly feeling relaxed has become a distant memory.

As my duties became more global, I found myself bouncing around numerous countries and infrequently at home in Berlin, Germany. Few places were truly relaxing to me. There was one place, however, where I was able to truly let down and have a good time. It was at our friend Linda's house. Her son Colin became my son's best friend when we moved to Germany.

At the first day of new student orientation at Berlin Brandenburg International School, my wife and I walked uneasily on the campus, desperately hoping our son would make a friend. Almost immediately on the playground, we ran into Linda. She was from the United Kingdom and had a beautiful northwestern London accent. Our son and Linda's son met and immediately took off for the playground. Second grade was off to a great start.

Before long, we found ourselves spending a lot of time together. When I was home, I loved going over to Linda's house in suburban Berlin. Linda's two children loved playing with our son. They jumped on a trampoline outside, played Star Wars, then would switch to playing Wii, and then they would run around shooting each other until eventually Colin and Christopher would get into a fight. Four-year-old Christopher would go find his mom so that Colin would get in trouble and his boo-boo would get kissed. The adults would sit around talking about expat life in Berlin, 80s British pop music, our mutual love for London, and the places we like to travel. We laughed a lot and always put on some good dance music.

Inevitably, it would be time for dinner and we would always eat spaghetti, which we all love. The three boys, like boys all over the world, would not stop talking and got very little of the food in their mouths. Eventually, we had to resort to threats as the parents cleaned off their plates while the kids had taken two bites at most—the spaghetti getting colder by the minute.

One evening, Linda put on Michael Jackson's "Thriller" and we all danced to it, children and parents. I did my Michael Jackson dance moves and the moonwalk; which I only do when I am truly comfortable with people. Colin said, "This is the best play-date ever!" And it was. We left that evening feeling our souls lifted, the stress temporarily gone, and as if everything was right in the world. A perfect afternoon and evening that made me forget about all the stresses and cares of the world.

That place of comfort and peace was a Muslim home. Linda and her husband are Muslims from England. Their parents were first-generation immigrants from Pakistan and India. But Linda and her husband were raised in middle-class England, on the industrial house music of the Manchester club scene. Neither are particularly religious, yet both are deeply moral, raising two very lovely boys. Linda's husband has an excellent job at a German pharmaceutical company, and Linda worked at a very respected politically conservative magazine. Other than their dietary restrictions, there was nothing to suggest that they were Muslims. No bowing to Mecca, no *Burkka*, no long beard, no affinity for terrorism, and no hostile words about the United States. In fact, both were deeply respectful of the fact that we were Christian missionaries. They spent no time preaching to us from the *Quran* or telling us about how they will one day take over the world. We were remarkably similar in many ways and were more likely to talk about the bad example that the cartoon *Spongebob Squarepants* sets for kids than we were about *Al-Qaeda* or 9/11. The funny things our children said and the constant messes they made were what the bulk of our conversations were about. How shocking it was, then, when my son spent some time in the United States and was told by Christians that all Muslims are evil. This made no sense to him, considering he spent much of his time on the playground and playing Minecraft with Colin, Hammad, and other Muslim children. The fact of the matter was that those portraying all Muslims as evil had never met one.

At the time of this writing, I have been traveling globally for my work for fifteen years. Due to the fact that I regularly travel to the Middle East and several of my colleagues live in Islamic countries, the troubles in the Middle East and the threat of militant Islam are very real to me. Unlike many of the readers of this book, my colleagues, my wife, my son, and I regularly need to enter into the Islamic world even if it is dangerous. We are willing to take that risk to do the Lord's work; however, the lesson we learn when we travel through the Middle East amidst the danger is not that all Muslims are evil. Quite the opposite is true; we see a nuance that is not visible in Western (particularly American) media. Most of us who have traveled, worked, or lived extensively in the Islamic world are struck by the friendliness of the people, their knowledge of politics and history, and the intellectual sophistication of many of the people we meet.

Yes, Islam is in crisis. The attacks on 9/11, the rise of the "Arab Spring," the resurgence of militant Islam, and the poor economic and political state of many Muslim societies is making this the most destabilized period in the Middle East in one hundred years. It is a crisis that most likely will last two generations and will completely reorder global society. Energy needs, water scarcity, military force, and immigration will be deeply affected by the Islamic world's troubles, and many of these troubles stem from Islam's tension with secular political order and the modern world. We are not witnessing a "Clash of Civilizations" as much as we are witnessing a clash within a civilization that is spilling out globally. Islamic civilization remains uncomfortable with modernity and many of its nations are filled with ethnic tension and sectarianism.

Regardless, the way forward is not about coming up with simplistic political opinions, theological statements, and poorly informed ideas that turn all Muslims into cartoon characters—no more representative of Christianity than the Ku Klux Klan. The diversity of the Islamic world, like the diversity of the Christian world is immense. And in this globalized, inner-connected world, we are far more likely to be living next to someone like Linda than we are to a terrorist.

Consequently, this book aims to introduce the reader to the Islamic world today, not shying away from its current challenges, but also beginning the process of humanizing Muslims. All are created in God's image according to Scripture, and if we love Muslims as ourselves, to paraphrase our personal Savior, Jesus, we will view them as part of the human family and God's creation. This book will deal honestly with the crisis within Islam and the myriad of key differences between Christianity and Islam, but it will not turn one and a half billion Muslims into cartoon caricatures that match the images propagated by ratings-obsessed news channels. Neither is this book meant to be a pamphlet on how to convert Muslims. The first step to presenting Christ is not coming up with our arguments, but first studying the culture and surveying the land. Despite intentionally being a short book for study and discussion in groups, this book aims to help the reader enter into the Islamic world and answer some of the most pressing questions Christians are asking during these difficult times.

If we are serious about engaging Muslims and bringing them to Christ, we cannot refuse to get to know them or have just a one-dimensional view of the Islamic world. Just as many Evangelicals resent Mormons or Jehovah's Witnesses knocking on our doors to tell us how wrong we are in not incorporating the ideas of Joseph Smith or Charles Taze Russell into our Christian faith, Muslims will never take too kindly to Christians confronting them without ever taking the time to understand their faith, their culture and their history. As any good missionary knows, we have to study the culture, make contact, and establish trust before truly engaging in dialogue with non-Christians. The reality in America, at least, is that the Christians who struggle the most with prejudice against Muslims have never lived with or known any Muslims personally. We need to do better if we are serious about sharing the love of Christ with Muslim brothers and sisters.

If there is one thing I ask of you it is to keep the story of Jesus and the woman at the well in your mind at all times (John 4:4–26). This is an important story about how Jesus asks us to get out of our prejudices and comfort zones in order to represent him. Jesus made a lot of unorthodox moves in that story. A good rabbi should never have been with that woman alone in the middle of the day. Neither should he have gone to Samaria, that land of heretics and blasphemers. Samaritans, like Muslims, were easy to caricaturize, and one could feel justified in shunning them and viewing them as a lost cause due to their heretical portrayal of God. But Jesus refused to do that. While he stayed true to his convictions, Jesus initiated a dialogue with the Samaritan woman and invited her to Living Water—not condemnation and demonization. This is the attitude that we must have when we engage Muslims. If we are truly confident that we possess the Living Water, then we need not resort to cheap shots, prejudice, and hatred. That's what insecure people do when they are afraid. If we truly believe that Jesus is the Way, then we need not be afraid.

CHAPTER 1

The Diversity of the Islamic World

There is a news story about another beheading done by the terrorist group ISIS as I sit down to write this first chapter of a book intended to help Christians understand what is happening in the world of Islam. ISIS, also known as IS (Islamic State) or ISIL (Islamic Syria and Levant, a name used to avoid recognizing ISIS as controlling a state), or *Daesh* in Arabic, is one of many militant groups that has flourished globally since the disintegration of Iraq and Syria as stable nation-states. There is also talk on the news today of ISIS and *Jabhat al-Nusra* joining forces to fight the moderate rebels, the Kurds, and the Americans as ISIS struggles to conquer all of Mesopotamia and create a true Islamic state. This makes for very scary headlines this morning.

But the reality is much more complicated than we will hear on the news, which tends to simplify everything into the most basic, most frightening sound bites possible. *Jabhat al-Nusra* and ISIS do not like each other one bit. ISIS has made it clear that it does not view *Jabhat al-Nusra* as Islamic and believes they are guilty of defection. This is because *Jabhat al-Nusra* was not willing to come under ISIS authority in April of 2013, and ISIS has claimed Caliphate status since June 29, 2014. It is actually a very small local group from *Jabhat al-Nusra* that is working alongside a small group from ISIS in the Qalamoun area, but the news will report this as a major alliance.

Actually, *Jabhat al-Nusra* is not even willing to view ISIS as legitimately holding a state, let alone a caliphate (i.e. having political and religious leadership of the Islamic world under a successor of the prophet Muhammad). This is one of the biggest problems for ISIS, the Americans trying to stabilize and/or democratize Islamic States, and anyone living or working in the Middle East. The diversity of opinions and divisions within the groups fighting in Iraq, Syria, and throughout the region is immense, complicated, and insurmountable. Surrounding both of these groups are many other militant groups, some *Sunni*, some *Shia*, some Kurdish, some hostile to Bashar Asaad's rapidly disintegrating Syrian secular *Ba'athist* state, others non-religious, and still others just seeking revenge and not interested in any kind of Islamic expansion.

Even within those groups forming alliances, divisions are so severe that if they were to win their battle against ISIS, they would then fracture and go to war with each other. Many of these "Islamic militias" are not even religious. In other words, in the West we tend to have a view of the Islamic world as being more unified, more powerful, and more spiritually in sync than it actually is in real life.

Consequently, this is where Christians studying Islam should begin: by understanding that we are dealing with an enormous religion, which like Christianity is filled with an incredible array of opinions, theologies, divisions, and conflicts. We must further acknowledge that what we hear in the news media and even among our churches and conversations with Christian friends simplifies these issues to an extreme degree. If the battle lines among angry, militant terrorist groups are this divided, imagine how diverse the Islamic world truly is when you factor in all one and a half billion Muslims, only 20 percent of whom live in Arab countries.

The Vast Islamic World

The Islamic world goes way beyond the countries of the Middle East or regions inhabited by Arabs. It stretches from the Far East of Indonesia (an island nation that stretches three thousand miles into the Pacific) to the far West Coast of Africa. Roughly half of the world, geographically speaking, has been deeply affected by Islamic faith and culture. But this Islam is rarely the Islam of Osama Bin Laden and ISIS. In Senegal, there are Muslims who worship a black prophet who came from the Atlantic Ocean—a clear mix of indigenous African religion and Islam. In one part of Indonesia there are Muslims who are pacifists and universalists; they believe in total non-violence and that everyone will go to heaven regardless of whether they are Muslims or not. In Algeria, Syria, and Albania, most of the people are extremely secular, atheists, or at least view religion as something that should be kept away from politics. Throughout Western Europe, there are second and third generation Muslims who care much more about secularism and Western pop culture than Islam, even though they are labeled "Muslims." And in the militant Islamic Republic of Iran led by the *Ayatollah* Khamenei, there are millions who have converted to Christianity or abandoned Islam altogether out of disgust for that democratic republic's hypocrisy and use of Islam in politics. In India, a predominantly Hindu nation and the world's largest democracy, millions of Muslims live peacefully alongside Christians and Hindus and have for centuries. Within the United States, some African Americans have been attracted to the Nation of Islam, a movement started in Detroit by Wallace Fard Muhammed. It is a movement considered heterodox by the vast majority of Muslims.

Islam is expressed very differently in different parts of the world. While some Muslim countries have had female Prime Ministers (Pakistan, Indonesia) others systematically oppress women

(Afghanistan). While some Muslims have been in long-time conflict with their neighbors (Iran, Iraq), others have co-existed with other ethnic groups in peace and harmony (Singapore, Malaysia, Lebanon). And while some countries have embraced a more austere form of Islam (Saudi Arabia, Iran), others have sought to keep religion and politics separate (Egypt, Syria, Iraq). In some countries, liberal democracy seems a long way off (Somalia, Sudan), while in others, it is in its early stages or showing real stability (Indonesia, Malaysia, Tunisia). Some Islamic countries are very poor with nearly non-existent economic development (Kyrgyzstan, Bangladesh) while others are very wealthy (United Arab Emirates, Qatar) and show exceptional economic growth and development (Turkey).

Within the Islamic world, as within Christianity (especially Protestantism), there are many different divisions. Just as a Roman Catholic from Guatemala may have little in common with an Eastern Orthodox Christian from Ukraine or a conservatively dressed Mennonite from Northern Indiana, hundreds of millions of Muslims have virtually nothing in common with each other. Some, like Saddam Hussein, are completely secular, while others may have been raised as secular communists in Albania or Yugoslavia. Still others may have been raised in cultures that were inherently products of "Islamic civilization." Just as atheists like Richard Dawkins or the late Christopher Hitchens were raised in "Christian" England, yet the religion failed to rub off on them and they are extremely secular—the same is true of some Muslims.

Clearly, many cultural, historical, demographic, economic, and political factors shape how Islam is expressed around the world, and these should not be minimized in favor of a one-size-fits all caricature of Islam. For the most part, many people are slow to truly commit time, energy, and money to dying to themselves for the sake of a religion. It is always the minority of believers who are deeply pious.

The Fastest Growing Religion in the World

Islam is currently the fastest growing religion in the world with approximately one and a half billion people falling under the broad categorization of "Muslim." This fact alarms Christians, but it should be remembered that much of this rapid growth is due to high-birth rates in Muslim countries. In some countries, anyone born is automatically labeled a Muslim. When Islam is the dominant faith, it is often the case that the vast majority of the people born are born into Muslim families, just as most Polish people are born into Roman Catholic families and may consider themselves "Catholic" or "Christian" whether they practice the faith or believe in it or not. This inflates the statistics because many uncommitted people, or people completely oblivious to the specifics of the faith, get labeled "Muslim."

The fastest growing religion *by conversion* is Christianity. And the Bible is by far and away the biggest selling or downloaded book in the world. Christianity is growing in places where it has traditionally not been known, unlike Islam, which does not spread cross-culturally as well as Christianity due to the fact that Christianity is not tied to any particular language or geographic location (an issue we will discuss in Chapter 3) the way Islam revolves around Arabia. Christian revivals in Vietnam, Mongolia, Nigeria, Brazil, China, and portions of India attest to the fact that Christianity is exceptionally good at crossing cultures and becoming an indigenous faith.

The Islamic world is also growing due to the investment made in expanding the faith and building mosques and Islamic Learning Centers throughout the world by wealthy Muslims from the Gulf States such as Saudi Arabia, Qatar, and the United Arab Emirates. New mosques are being constructed in North America, Latin America, Africa, Asia, and Australia. In the United Kingdom, mosques are constructed constantly while Christian churches regularly close. But many of these mosques cater to Muslim communities that are already established, usually among ethnic groups that are primarily Muslim.

Birth rates in Islamic nations such as Pakistan, Bangladesh, and Iran (which have traditionally been very high) are dropping quickly. Much of this is due to women entering the workforce, the rise of the global middle-class, and a better understanding of birth control. Currently, the Arab world is experiencing what is known as a "youth bulge," when the population of young people is exceptionally high. In many Middle Eastern countries, 50 percent of the population is under 25. This is extremely dangerous and destabilizing for societies, and this is one of the primary reasons the Middle East is currently in crisis. Testosterone-fueled males with no education, no economic prospects, and no sexual outlets can easily be recruited into a life of revolution and/or militancy.

Nevertheless, the combination of slowing birthrates and the bad reputation that politicized Islam is gaining around the world could easily lead to a decline in the growth of Islam in the near future. The chances of the next generation of Muslims being far more secular is very high—hence the concern of groups such as the Taliban, the Ayatollahs of Iran, Al-Qaeda, and ISIS. The strength of the Islamic militant movement is often overestimated. Overall, across the board, the world is secularizing as global income levels are rising. This affects Christianity, Judaism, and Islam as well as local indigenous folk religions around the world, which have already been in steep decline over the past century.

Divisions within Islam

There are many divisions within the Islamic faith, more than can be discussed in this short book. Nevertheless, some of the primary divisions between the various sects of Islam are vital to understand.

While most Muslims share certain core beliefs (such as a belief in *Allah*, the sacred nature of the *Quran*, and the importance of practicing the Five Pillars of Islam), they have varying beliefs about authority, the role of religion and politics, theology, the interpretation of Islamic law, and the importance of certain prophets, Islamic thinkers, and religious leaders.

The most well known division in Islam is between *Sunni* Muslims, who constitute 85 percent of all Muslims, and *Shia* Muslims, who make up 15 percent. This division goes back to the time of Muhammad's death in 632 CE. When the prophet died, it was not clear who should be the leader, and it was understood that no one could ever take his place or become the next prophet. Nevertheless, someone needed to be the leader of this fast-growing faith.

***Sunni* Islam:** *Sunnis* (followers of the *Sunnah*, which means *example*) passed the mantle of leadership to a *Caliph* (successor), who would be a political and military leader, but not a prophet like Muhammad. The first *Caliph* was Muhammad's father-in-law, Abu Bakr. He was not chosen by hereditary succession, but rather because he was pious, wise, and loyal to Muhammed.

***Shia* Islam:** The *Shias* (Party of Ali) are mostly found in present day Iraq, Iran, Bahrain, and Lebanon. *Shia* Islam was opposed to the elevation of Abu Bakr, arguing that succession in leadership should be hereditary. None of Muhammad's sons survived childhood, consequently the leader (or *Imam*) should have been the husband of Muhammad's daughter Fatima, a man named Ali. Ali was forced to wait 35 years before becoming the leader and was assassinated shortly thereafter. Over the course of history, the outnumbered *Shia* would feel maligned, dominated, and disrespected by the dominant *Sunnis*. *Shia* history, then, is filled with sadness and a concern for the end of oppression and the restoration of justice in the world. *Shias* look toward the future with anticipation and the past with a heavy heart. This is in contrast to the *Sunni* Muslims who were dominant in Islamic history and tend to celebrate, remember, and romanticize the glory days of the Islamic Empire.

But even within *Shia* Islam, there was a split over the number of *Imams* who succeeded Muhammed. The *Zaydis* recognized five, the *Ismailis* recognized seven, and the *Ithna Ashari* recognized twelve. *Ithna Ashari* is by far the most numerous and is prominent in Iran. Some readers may recall that the former President of Iran referred to the return of the "Twelfth *Imam*." This is because the twelfth *Imam*, Muhammad al-Muntazar disappeared in 874 CE as a child without sons. Unable to produce a successor, the belief is that the Twelfth *Imam* is currently hiding and will return at the end of time to prove the truth of *Shia* Islam and bring about a perfect Islamic society. Until then, it is up to the *mullahs* (*Shia* clergy) to interpret Islamic law, and at the top is the supreme religious leader known as the *Ayatollah*.

As we can see, the division between *Sunni* and *Shia* originated as a political one, unlike the theological division between the Eastern Orthodox Church and the Roman Catholic Church in the Great Schism of 1054 CE.

Wahhabi **Islam:** *Wahhabi* Islam has become more well known in the United States since the 9/11 attacks. This is because the hijackers came from Saudi Arabia, and *Wahhabi* Islam is the dominant form of Islamic faith in that Arab Kingdom. However, it is important to note that key planners of the 9/11 attacks were Egyptian, Lebanese, and Baluchi, and most were from a Sunni background.[1] Today, *Wahhabi* Islam can be said to be a form of *Sunni* Islam although it didn't start out that way. It is a very austere form of Islam named after a scholar of Islamic law and theology in Mecca and Medina named Muhammad Ibn Abd al-Wahhab (1703–1791). Frustrated by the continuing worship of pagan gods and moral laxness found

---

1. Juan Cole, *Engaging the Muslim World* (New York: Palgrave MacMillan), 84.

in Central Arabia, Wahhab preached a return to literalism and a rejection of medieval Islamic law that he viewed as corrupt. In other words, he was an 18ᵗʰ century fundamentalist who wanted to go back to the *Quran*, Muhammad, and Muhammad's example. He rejected all the theological innovations and discussions that had happened since the time of Muhammad.

Wahhabi Islam was far less tolerant than other forms of Islam at the time. Along with a tribal chief named Muhammad Ibn Saud, Wahhab oversaw a movement that violently conquered much of Arabia for *Wahhabi* Islam. This included the destruction of pagan shrines and the *Shia* pilgrimage site at Karbala (in modern Iraq) that housed the tomb of Hussein. This offense has never been forgotten by the *Shia* and helps to explain why modern day Saudi Arabia has such a hostile relationship with modern-day Iraq and Iran.

Eventually, *Wahhabi* Islam became the official interpretation of the modern-day country of Saudi Arabia. Around the world Saudi Arabia's Islam is known for using harsh criminal punishment such as cutting off hands or stoning people, preventing foreign religious beliefs from being expressed, insisting that women be completely covered at all times outside of their homes, forbidding women from driving, and being legalistic and practicing literalism.

While *Wahhabi* Islam is indeed strict, a few things should be noted: 1) *Wahhabi* believers in Bahrain do not have the same, strict sensibility. 2) Saudi Arabia is home to the two most holy sites in Islam (Mecca and Medina), and usually the closer you are to the religious birthplace of a movement, the more militant the belief. 3) Only 62 percent of Saudis describe themselves as religious. The extreme mixing of politics and religion invariably leads to a decline in religious belief, as it has in *Shia* Iran.[2]

---

2. "The Saudi Public Speaks: Religion, Gender, and Politics," International Journal of Middle East Studies, 214.

Sufi **Islam:** *Sufi* is a mystical tradition within Islam that aims to discipline the mind and body in order to experience the presence of God. Unlike the Christian monastic tradition, *Sufis* do not remove themselves from the world but practice something known as the "greater *jihad*" which is an attempt to control one's own sinful nature and instead study, meditate, pray, fast, and seek the will of *Allah. Sufi* Islam was a corrective movement that arose to critique the materialism that was starting to infest many Muslims during the Umayyad Caliphate (661-750 CE). Also, unlike many Christian monastics, *Sufi* Muslims engage in political involvement and missionary work to a high degree.

Sufi believers also tend to believe that they are practicing the true form of Islam and are often opposed by *Wahhabi* and S*alafi* Muslims. Iran, Pakistan, and Turkey are three Islamic countries that have little tolerance for *Sufi* Islam, and there are many cases of *Sufi* shrines being attacked and destroyed. Some Muslims view *Sufi* as too far removed from orthodox Islam and influenced by pagan or foreign religious influences. Many Westerners who take up Islam, on the other hand, join *Sufi* Islam, which to Westerners, can feel like a peaceful form of Buddhism, not a hostile, militant, and terror-obsessed movement.

There are many other movements within Islam including *Salafi*[3] and *Khawarij*[4] that can be studied, but it is clear from our review that there are significant divisions within Islam that in many ways are much more personal and certainly longer than the division between some Islamic nations and the West. All of this creates volatility within Islam that is important for us to internalize before we

---

3. **Salafism** is sometimes considered identical to Wahhabi Islam, but seems to have been heavily influenced by post-1960 fundamentalist movements. Salafi believers can be found primarily in the Gulf nations such as Saudi Arabia, United Arab Emirates, and Qatar.

4. **Kharjites** are Muslims who initially supported the succession of Muhammed's son-in-law but then rejected his leadership. Kharijites have little tolerance for Muslims who continue to live in sin or believe the wrong theology. They are concerned with just rulers and put a strong emphasis on martyrdom.

jump to the conclusion that Islam's primary fight is against the West or other religions. The fact of the matter is that the differences and feuds within Islam are severe, long-standing, and have proven to be irreparable thus far. We will now turn to the origins of Islam and see that the Islamic faith began on a soil that was full of conflict and tribal warfare from its inception.

Discussion Questions

1. How would you characterize your view of Islam? How does it compare with your view of Buddhism, Judaism, Hinduism, or other major religions? What has primarily formed your opinion?

2. Have you ever been close friends with a Muslim, had one who was an acquaintance, or lived among Muslim people? How did they or did they not fit the Western stereotypes of Muslims being violent and hostile toward anything non-Muslim?

3. Often it is erroneously believed that the world's Muslims are a unified force. What kind of diverse forms of theology, governance, and practices do you see in this chapter?

4. Have you ever traveled to a Muslim country? What were your observations regarding what was different and what was the same between those countries and your country? Have you been to two or more Islamic countries? How were they similar to each other and how were they different?

5. What kind of prejudices or stereotypes do you think Muslims have of Western Christians? How would you convince a Muslim that those views are not true? Should they accept your explanation? Why or why not?

6. Name different Christian denominations or branches and observe some of the differences and diversity. How would you explain these differences to a Muslim?

CHAPTER

Who Was Muhammad?

The speed at which Islam became a major world religion is nothing short of astonishing. In 632 CE, Islam was a minor religious movement in the distant sands of underdeveloped Arabia. Within one hundred years, the new religion would extend from eastern Central Asia all the way to Spain and North Africa, absorbing great empires and displacing Persian, Greek, Latin, and Berber with the "holy language" of Arabic. Local folk religions and ancient texts and traditions were replaced by the *Quran* and Arab cultural values. This obscure desert reformation would grow to be the core foundation of a civilization still visible today. All of this can be traced to one man, Muhammad ibn Abdullah, born in 570 CE.

Arabia and Religion in the Time of Muhammad

The Arabian Peninsula was a land of Bedouin tribes and traders. It was a rough environment—a desert region peopled with nomadic clans, or *hayy*, each attempting to avoid annihilation at the hands of stronger clans. Without a central authority or government, tribes served as a form of protection in this hostile environment. Temporary alliances and truces would form, and then be revoked later. Located on a major global trade route, tribes traded with, and raided peoples from throughout the Middle East, North Africa, and Central Asia. Broken agreements or betrayals were never forgotten and a culture of vendettas existed. Life was dangerous, violent, and unjust.

Arabia was a land where the people believed in many gods and goddesses and in spirits who dwelled in trees, stones, and other inanimate objects. Arabia had not produced any complex theologies such as those found in Judaism and Christianity, or other Eastern faiths. The city of Mecca, however, possessed a central shrine to the gods known as the *Kabah*, a cube shaped shrine that houses a black rock that most likely came from a meteorite. In Muhammad's time, the *Kabah* shrine was filled with 360 idols of deities from which the various tribes would seek protection. While the ancient shrine was most likely built for a particular ancient deity, by the time of Muhammad's life, the Supreme God was known as *Allah* (which simply means "God"), and Arabs would make a pilgrimage (*hajj*) to circle the shrine seven times, kiss the black stone, and perform a few other rituals nearby.

Muhammad, we are told, was a pious man. He was a merchant, but he also cared deeply about spiritual matters. In addition to participating in the *hajj*, Muhammad prayed, gave to the poor, fasted, and spent time contemplating the spiritual condition of his people, particularly his tribe of successful merchants, the *Quraysh*. Muhammad was concerned about the spirit of materialism and selfishness that had engulfed the people, and particularly about their lack of concern for the poor and for justice. As harsh as Arab society was with its tribalism and vendettas, there was also a strong strain of hospitality that was important as it helped people to survive in such a harsh climate. The desert had few resources, and that required violence and pillaging. At the same time, the desert was so inhospitable, it also required a culture of hospitality. To this day, Arabs and others throughout the Islamic world care about hospitality to a great degree and often surprise Westerners who visit the region with their graciousness to visitors. It is a trait of which they are very proud. Muhammad felt that people were moving away from this more communal attitude as people got wealthier and less interested in looking out for each other. A spiritual reform was needed, in his opinion.

Muhammad also seems to have been self-conscious about how developed theologically Christianity and Judaism were in comparison to the religious practices of his corner of Arabia. The Christians and Jews had holy books, engaging stories, extensive codes of ethics, a rich history, a civilization heritage, and theological complexity. The faith practices of the Arabs in comparison seemed primitive, superstitious, and ineffective. It seemed to be pagan polytheism at its most basic. He respected and admired the stories of the Jews and Christians. In time, Muhammad would continue to praise and lift up many of the stories and prophets from Christian and Hebrew scriptures, but he would sometimes get the details wrong and be ridiculed by the Jews. Eventually, their rejection caused him to become disillusioned. He would also eventually become confused by the theological inconsistency of the Christians who were always arguing and fighting with each other over who Jesus was and how Christianity should be practiced. The lack of unity between Christians led Muhammad to become frustrated with Christianity.

Muhammad's Revelation

According to Muslims, Muhammad's revelation occurred when he was praying in a cave in Mount Hira near Mecca during the month of Ramadan in 610 CE. He was startled awake by a presence that frightened him, and he began to recite words given to him from *Allah*. These would be the first verses of the *Quran*.

It is interesting to note that unlike in Christianity when the Spirit fills Stephen or the apostles, Muhammad actually felt fear when he encountered divinity and dreaded these moments of revelation. One can find the same sentiment in other faiths such as Tibetan Buddhism or Haitian Voodoo. Unlike in Christianity, in other faiths when a spirit fills someone, it is terrifying; and this was the case with the Islamic Prophet.

Muhammad only shared about these revelations with his wife Khadija and her cousin who was a Christian. They felt that these revelations were authentic and believed in Muhammad. It took two years for him to feel ready to begin preaching, but once he did, he gained converts very quickly. Among the first converts were his cousin Ali ibn Abi Talib and his father-in-law Abu Bakr who would play important roles later in the development and continuation of the Islamic faith. Muhammad's message of care for the poor and greater equality resonated with some of the people of his *Quraysh* tribe. From his point of view, he was not really preaching a new religion (which would have been quite audacious in those times before the radical individualism of today), but was calling people back to the one true God—the one the Jews and Christians preached about. He was primarily calling people back to monotheism. Muhammad did not teach that all other prophets found in Judaism and Christianity (including Jesus) were wrong. On the contrary, he was simply the prophet *Allah* had raised to call back the *Quraysh* and to call Arabia back to order. The way the reordering would take place, however, would have huge ramifications, as we shall soon see.

In the same way that the Christian story was transmitted orally before it was written down, Arabia had many illiterate people (including Muhammad) who received their teachings from Muhammad's preaching and eventually through the reciting of the *Quran's* verses twenty years later.

Muhammad's followers were known as "Muslims," people who practiced full surrender to *Allah* ("*Islam*" means surrender). It was vital that a new faith community, known as *Ummah*, be formed that would bring justice to all and honor God. This became an important development in Islam in that honoring God meant ushering in a new society here on Earth, not sometime in the afterlife. While Jesus spoke of the kingdom of God being present and called his followers to represent that Kingdom, for Islam, *earthly political* reform was paramount. The expectation was that the *Ummah* would have a cause or struggle (*jihad*) that it was always fighting for together. Clear earthly reform needed to take place, and where Jesus made several comments that made it clear that his Kingdom "is not of this world" (John 18:36), it was the job of Muslims to usher in a new society immediately. In the New Testament, Jesus turned over tables and cleared out the temple to show how the temple-based faith had been corrupted, but that was a one-time event. In Islam, the cause of the faith would be to do that in perpetuity, turning over all temples, even if it included being at war. So the reordering of this world did not necessarily mean that Muhammad viewed himself as the only prophet, but it did mean that his mandate to usher in a revolution was the final word, and that revolution would be absolute and eventually would include violence, if necessary.

The creation of this new community was revolutionary in another way. In Arabia, tribal identity was everything, but Muhammad ended up creating an affiliation of tribal groups that were bound by his teachings instead of bloodlines. This was a radical innovation that meant universal ethics could be transmitted across tribes, as opposed to limited within one small group. A large "tribe" could be formed based on faith, not on tribal identity. The point at which this unification came about is known as the *Hijrah* (622 CE). These first tribes that signed on were from *Yathrib,* which we now know as the holy city of Medina where Muhammad died in 632 CE. This new faith-movement, which grew rapidly under Muhammad's leadership, opened the door for tribalism to break down and eventually for millions to unite as a potent force under the banner of Islam.

Battles, Death, and Succession

Muhammad's preaching was accepted by some and rejected by others. His teachings on hell were frightening to people and the logical consequence of his teaching was that people's ancestors were condemned to damnation if they had been polytheists while alive. Since this was often the case, it was a bitter pill for followers to swallow. His attacks on materialism and injustice threatened those who were profiting from the imbalanced society. And Jews and Christians found his accounts of their Scriptures to be riddled with errors.

By 616 CE Muhammad's relations with his own clan the *Quraysh* had deteriorated so badly that no one was allowed to trade or marry Muhammad's followers. Persecution ensued and Muhammad's revered wife Khadija died. Muhammad's uncle and tribal protector Abu Talib died as well. Talib had raised the orphan Muhammad whose parents had passed away when he was an infant. But by 622 CE, a number of tribes, including some that were adherents of Judaism, joined Muhammad and his friend Abu Bakr in their religious movement. Muhammad married several wives, practicing polygamy. It was common to do so for political accommodation with the tribes that had decided to join him. Muslims may point out to non-Muslims that Muhammad's view of women was actually more elevated and liberal than that of Arab society at a time when women were viewed as less important than camels. Muhammad limited the amount of wives men could have to four and insisted that they must be able to properly take care of their material needs. This was progress in that society.

In 624 CE, Muhammad and his followers led a raid against a caravan and the *Quraysh* retaliated. The Battle of Badr in 624 CE became legend when the vastly outnumbered Muslims defeated the *Quraysh* handily. The Muslims then suffered a significant defeat in the Battle of Uhud 625 CE, but then had a resounding victory in the Battle of the Trench in 627 CE. The third "miraculous" battle led many to view Muhammad as a true warrior and prophet, and the numbers of his believers grew.

Warfare was brutal in Arabia and it was a winner-take-all attitude. Soldiers, as well as women and children, could be slaughtered. From the point of view of the Arabs, allowing them to live would mean that the vendetta would be in place, and they would come back for revenge in the future. This pattern of fear of retribution and total destruction can be seen in the current crisis in Iraq and Syria where there is a constant fear of what would happen if the power were to shift and one particular defeated sect were to make a comeback.

As with the status of women, many Muslims and scholars will argue that Muhammad's approach to violence was actually more temperate and contemporary than the West often portrays. He had moments when he sought peace, protested without violence, and asked for the protection of women, children, and unbelievers. Many instances of his more civil attitude are cited, including when Muhammad took Mecca without killing anyone. By uniting the tribes under the banner of Islam, it can be said that Muhammad actually began the process of ending the cycles of extreme violence that were engulfing all of the Arabian Peninsula.

When Muhammad died in 632 CE, a decision needed to be made about who would lead the community and what form it would take. Muhammad's father-in-law Abu Bakr believed that the *Ummah* would need to continue in unity and under a single ruler. Some argued for Muhammad's young cousin Ali ibn Abi Talib to be the first *Caliph*—the leader and successor to the prophet Muhammad—but Abu Bakr won the vote and went about consolidating the *Ummah's* power and was influential in keeping less religious tribes in the fold and leading successful military incursions into the neighboring Sassanid Persian and Byzantine Empires. His successful reign lasted only two years, however, as he became ill and died.

Sunni Muslims revere Abu Bakr, but *Shia* Muslims believe that Bakr should never have become *Caliph*. They believe that Muhammad's cousin Ali ibn Abi Talib should have had the Caliphate. When Persia became the independent state of Iran in 1501, *Shiism* became the official religion of the empire. This old division in Islam was exploited in order for Iran to carve out an identity separate from the other *Sunni* Islamic states and empires. Tremendous hostility exists between *Sunni* and *Shii* lands to this day.

The first *Caliph*, Abu Bakr; was followed by Umar I. He greatly expanded the Islamic world and allowed Jews and Christians to keep their faith. He was assassinated by the Persians in retribution for Islam's rapid expansion into Persia. Umar I was followed by Uthman who was assassinated in an uprising, and he was followed by Ali ibn Abi Talib who was also assassinated.

Different dynasties emerged over the years, but the caliphate ended in the modern era with the collapse of the Ottoman Empire. The secular first president of the modern Turkish Republic, Mustafa Atatürk, abolished the caliphate in 1924.

On June 29, 2014, ISIS and their leader Abu Bakr al-Baghdadi declared that the worldwide caliphate had returned with al-Baghdadi as the *Caliph*. This "historical moment" rallied many thousands of Muslims from around the world to Iraq and Syria to be part of the newly-formed Islamic State (IS). The *Caliph* claims political, military, and religious authority over all Muslims; however, no Islamic nation or Islamic scholars have recognized Bakr as Muhammad's rightful successor. Only other terrorist organizations have sanctioned this caliphate. The caliphate promises to usher in a new, better Islamic society, but so far, that has not occurred. Instead, the territory it has possessed has been won through torture, beheadings, rape, and pillage. Unable to provide for the people it has conquered, the Islamic State will have a hard time convincing most Muslims around the world that a new and just Islamic order has been established on Earth. Another option would be for ISIS to claim that its caliphate is only meant to be the beginning of an apocalyptic final battle, in which case, its current ineffectiveness could be justified. Both those against ISIS and those siding with the terrorists will appeal to the life of Muhammad and the teachings of the *Quran* to make their case.

Discussion Questions

1. What was pre-Islamic Arabian culture like? How might that have impacted Islam? How has Christianity been shaped by culture?

2. What adjustments was Muhammad seeking to make to Arab tribal Society?

3. How is Jesus' understanding of the kingdom of God different from Muhammad's understanding of God's role in this world?

4. Muhammad was interested in Christianity but found that there was too much disagreement among Christians. Do you think this is a weakness for Christianity today or a strength?

5. In what ways was Muhammad a progressive reformer? Why is Islam not viewed as progressive today? What do you think happened?

CHAPTER

The Basics of Islam

The subject of Islam is one that is enormous. For the purpose of this intentionally short book—which aims to help the reader understand some of the current events occurring in the Islamic World—all that can be offered is the most basic introduction to the primary beliefs and practices of the faith.

Perhaps the most important point to understand about Islam is that unlike Christianity, which elevates Jesus Christ and his life as the central figure and moment of revelation upon which all else hinges, Islam does not elevate a person, but rather a book: the *Quran*. In other words, for Christians the hinge of history and salvation is centered on Christ's incarnation and resurrection, while for Muslims it is about those verses given to Muhammad by *Allah*. While fundamentalist Christians may believe the Word of God is inspired, it is still understood to have been given to particular men (Paul, Luke, John, and so forth) who then wrote it down though their personal letters, poetry, or history. The *Quran*, however, is believed to be the direct words of God.

The Quran

Unlike the Bible, the *Quran* is not a collection of narratives, poems, laws, letters, and history. In fact, to non-Muslims, the *Quran* can seem dull and repetitive. Its content is to be recited out loud, and it is said that it is beautiful to listen to when recited in Arabic. It is a small book compared to the Bible, consisting of 114 chapters (*surahs*) and six thousand verses, of which the main thrust is that there is only one God (*Allah*).

The *Quran* honors the Jewish prophets and acknowledges that Moses received the Law from God. Abraham, Moses, and Jesus are all revered as men of *Allah*, but Muhammad is the one who received the most important revelation. It calls the Jews and Christians "People of the Book" but accuses the Jews and Christians of breaking their solemn pledge to *Allah* and forgetting many important aspects of the faith (Surah 5:10-14).[5]

The Quran teaches monotheism and Jesus is honored as a great prophet, but he is not considered to be God's final prophet and is not believed to have been crucified and resurrected. In a shame-based culture such as that of Arabia, Christ's manner of death is humiliating and unacceptable. The *Quran* says: *However, they did not slay him, and neither did they crucify him, but it only seemed to them [as if it had been so]* (4:157).

Arising out of polytheistic Arabia, Islam condemns the idea of the Trinity which they believe means worshiping three Gods instead of Allah: *"Believe then, in God and His apostles, and do not say, a trinity. Desist for your own good. God is but One God; utterly remote is He, in His glory, from having a son: unto Him belongs all that is in the heavens and all that is on earth and none is as worthy of trust as God"* (4:171).

Unlike the Bible which can (and should) be translated into all languages; the *Quran* is only considered the *Quran* when it is in Arabic. Arabic is the language of Islam, and one must learn to read and recite Arabic to be a good Muslim according to the *Quran*: *"These are messages of a revelation clear in itself and clearly showing the truth. Behold, We have bestowed it from on high as a discourse in the Arabic tongue, so that you might encompass it with your reason* (12:1-2). Other *surahs*

---

5. Muhammad Asad, trans., *The Message of the Quran: The Full Account of the Revealed Arabic Text Accompanied by Parallel Transliteration* (London: The Book Foundation, 2003).

also highlight the importance of Arabic (12:1, 12:2, 20:113, 39:28, 41:3, 41:44, 42:7, and 43:3). This has huge implications, not the least of which is that many Muslims around the world do not know what is actually in the *Quran*. Furthermore, even if they do learn to read and recite it in Arabic, they may not really understand what they are reading. This is a very big problem in Islam. The book is revered, but millions do not have it touch them at their core being or in their heart-language. Many who join terrorist groups such as ISIS may not have even read the *Quran* or understood it.

Christianity on the other hand was designed to be inherently global. The importance of this cannot be underestimated. In Acts 2, the Day of Pentecost makes it clear that the Christian message will be accessible in multiple languages. This sets the stage for the true globalization of Christianity that occurs after Antioch as recorded in the Book of Acts. Since language is a culture's primary source of identity, the ability to speak, think, write, and communicate overall with God and engage His Word in one's own primary language leads to a deep internalizing of the faith. It also breaks down the idea that any language or culture (such as Arabic culture and language) is superior to any other. Imagine how limited we would be if every Christian around the world had to speak and read in Aramaic to understand God's Word! Furthermore, it means that the spread and transmission of Christianity can be more global and involve more contextualization and integration than Islam. That is why we see Christianity in a greater diversity of cultures than Islam. Christianity has exploded in China, Nigeria, and Guatemala, for instance. These three countries have nothing in common with each other, but each has embraced Christianity and made it their own in large numbers. Islam, on the other hand, is centered in and around Arabia—a culture difficult for most of the world to relate to because of its unique history, geography, and culture. Some may want to quarrel with this description, but there is simply no religion in the world that has an easier time of embedding itself in radically different cultures than Christianity. The *Quran* does not have this key flexibility.

The Quran and Violence

The question of whether Islam is an inherently violent religion will be addressed in Chapter 5 because it is this author's belief that the foundational ethos and early years of Islam created a culture comfortable with violence and rigidity that is not easily critiqued or reformed from within Islam. It is important to note, however, that the *Quran* has admonitions against unnecessary violence as well as calls for vengeance. Initially, Muhammad had chosen the path of non-violence as he spread his message and won converts. He and his followers suffered persecution in Mecca and when he eventually solidified his power-base, the new revelations gave him the authority to fight.

In *Surah* 22, for instance, permission is given to those who fight because they have been wronged: *"Permission [to fight] is given to those against whom war is being wrongfully waged—and verily, God has indeed the power to succour them"* (*Surah* 22:39).

But then *Surah* 16:125 says: *"Call though [all mankind] unto the Sustainer's path with wisdom and godly exhortation, and argue with them in the most kindly manner."*

Surah 2:192 reminds Muslims that *"God is much-forgiving, a dispenser of Grace."* But the next *surah* immediately after that says: *"Hence, fight against them until there is no more oppression and all worship is devoted to God alone"* (*Surah* 2:193). The reality is that even though there are many passages calling on Muslims to fight the non-believer, they are often surrounded by other passages that call for restraint. It can sound schizophrenic to non-Muslims, but this is the same argument made against Christian scriptures.

Islamic militants cling to portions such as *Surah* 5:33:

"It is but a just recompense for those who make war on God and His apostle, and endeavor to spread corruption on earth, that they are being slain in great numbers, or crucified in great numbers, or have, in result of their perverseness, their hands and feet cut off in great numbers, or are being [entirely] banished from [the face of] the earth: such is their ignominy in this world."

But most Muslims will argue that these verses have been taken out of context and that Islam sides with the peaceful verses.

Muslims can also point to the verses in the Bible such as Exodus 15:3 (KJV), *"The Lord is a man of war: the Lord is his name."* or Deuteronomy 7:2, *"And when the Lord your God has delivered them over to you and you have defeated them, then you must destroy them totally. Make no treaty with them, and show them no mercy."* They may also point out verses such as *"Happy is the one who seizes your infants and dashes them against the rocks"* (Ps 137:9) or the fact that the city of Ai is completely massacred in Joshua, Chapter 8. Christians will argue that these verses are taken out of context, but the verses in the *Quran* about violence are more open-ended. Inevitably, the conversation ends in a stalemate.

The persecution and attacks on Muhammad and his followers opened the door to an early development of a form of just-violence doctrine for Islam. Muhammad and his followers were allowed to retaliate and seek retribution when attacked. Chapter 5 will discuss how this comfort with militancy grew in Islam due to certain factors not present in Christianity. For now, it is important to note that as in Christianity, Muslims can point to verses that highlight tolerance as well as violence. Many times, when a Muslim says that the *Quran* preaches against violence, they mean this as much as a Christian does when they say the same thing about the Bible. Muslims view the revelation as pointing toward peace just as Christians do. Others choose to view those violent Scriptures as authoritative. For Christians, the sum of all Christian theology in the life and witness of Christ provides an important critique and frame of reference for everything in our Christian scriptures, because the Word became Flesh. Islam has no such move, so another way was needed to deal with those verses.

The Doctrine of Abrogation and the Haddith

The *Quran* can often seem to contradict itself. This presented a challenge for Muslims on how to interpret the verses, so the Doctrine of Abrogation was formed which gave ultimate authority to those verses that came later to Muhammad. As we have seen, the more Muhammad and the Muslims were challenged, the more he received revelations that retaliation was acceptable. Some scholars would suggest that verses were given later to make corrections because the Muslims were initially not ready for the full revelation; the verses were parceled out over time so they could be understood and implemented.

The *Quran* is also quite repetitive and does not cover a wide array of topics the way the Bible does. As Islam continued to grow and build an empire, the *Ummah* needed more clarity about what Muhammad had said or what he would do in particular situations. The *Quran* does not offer as much guidance on how a community of believers should act, as do the Old and New Testaments for Jews and Christians. There is not a clear personal code of ethics, for instance. Consequently, the *Haddith* was developed and its justification is found in the Quran in *Surah* 2:151 when *Allah* says that he will impart wisdom. "Wisdom" came to mean this extra source of revelation based on the life of Muhammad. This is actually contradictory because Muhammad is to be viewed as an ordinary man who is merely a source of revelation. Nevertheless, with the development of the *Haddith*, Muhammad's status is elevated in a way that it should not be.

During the period of the Abaassids (750-935 CE), a man from Gaza, Egypt, named Muhammad Idris Ibn al-Shafii, argued that Muhammad had not only recited the *Quran* but also interpreted for everyone how to act it out. People should look to the verified sayings and actions of the prophets as recorded by recognized Muslim authorities who were able to trace their relationships directly back to the Prophet. Short narrative, oral traditions were circulated about Muhammad and only when they were written down did these teachings become *Haddith*. They were then classified in a variety of ways to determine which traditions were revelatory or for guidance and which were not. Other holy men joined in this effort, and a more complete picture of how Muhammad had acted and behaved became available.

While open criticism, textual criticism, and debates on the Quran are not as prevalent as they are in Christianity, the *Haddith* does have a tradition of being scrutinized by Muslims. This also includes disputes about versions of the *Haddith* and the differences between them, which is a point of contention between *Sunni* and *Shia*. The combination of the many *Haddith* that developed and the *Quran* made it possible to create a more complete understanding of what life in the Islamic world should be like.

Sharia

This led to the development of *Sharia*, which simply means "law." (Non-Westerners often make the mistake of saying "Sharia Law" which is redundant.) While Christianity is more concerned with correct theological belief, Islam, like Judaism, is more concerned about correct behavior. Muslim's day-to-day beliefs are derived from *Sharia* and *Haddith* more than the *Quran*, which is one of the reasons why condemning violence in Islam is not very easy. Eventually, different schools of law were formed and viewed as valid. As with the creation of Christian theology between the time of Christ and the present day, Islamic theological history is far more complex and diverse than non-Muslims today think. In the same way the early church had councils that developed new doctrines and theological language that led to reformations and counter-reformations, Islam has its own long history of debate and development. The images on television are of a very monolithic, simple-minded faith, but in actuality, there were countless schools of Islam, including movements and counter-movements that led to tremendous diversity.

Sunni Muslims, for instance, derive *Sharia* from four sources: 1) the *Quran,* 2) the *Sunnah*—the example of Muhammad as found in the *Haddith,* 3) *Qiyas*—which gives parallels between similar situations or principles when no clear text is found in the Quran or Sunnah, and 4) consensus, known as *Ijma,* which is based on the belief that Muslims will be able to completely agree. In reality, this has been impossible without a clergy, which Islam does not have. Consequently, *Ulamas,* or scholars who study the *Quran* and *Haddith,* were formed. There are four major schools of law that developed. Some focused more on the *Quran*, others on the *Haddith*, and others on *Ijma*. These different emphases lead to different variations on the law that could be quite different.

The *Hanafi* School of Law is more liberal and allows Muslims to marry people outside of the faith. It is more dependent on *Qiya* and can be commonly found in Turkey, Lebanon, Syria, Jordan, Egypt, the Balkans, Central Asian countries, and countries in the Asian sub-continent such as India and Bangladesh, as well as in China among its Muslim minorities.

The *Maliki* School of Law depends heavily on the *Haddith* and can be found in Egypt, North Africa, Kuwait, Qatar, Bahrain, United Arab Emirates, and some parts of Saudi Arabia.

The *Shafi'i* in Arabia focuses more on *Ijma* and the consensus it brings and is found in Somalia, Ethiopia, Djibouti, Kenya, among the Kurds, Palestine, Indonesia, Malaysia, Sri Lanka, Singapore, Thailand, Brunei, the Philippines, and other areas in Asia.

The *Hanbali* focuses on a very extreme, literal interpretation of the *Quran,* doesn't even acknowledge Muslims in other schools, and is mostly found in the Gulf nations such as Saudi Arabia, Oman, and the United Arab Emirates. The very militant *Wahabbi* Muslims of Saudi Arabia are an example.

In addition to these *Sunni* schools, there are other schools in Shia Islam (which does have clergy) as well as other schools of Law among smaller Islamic sects.

Sharia greatly affects daily life—particularly family life. Whether women should be completely veiled or drive cars, or whether people can drink alcohol or marry a non-Muslim, as well as many other daily practices, will depend on which school of *Sharia* is being practiced. Many Muslims primarily live under the laws of Western-inspired legal codes and do not adhere to *Sharia.* It's important to note that many Muslims in the United States do not live under *Sharia* and do not want to live under *Sharia.* They greatly enjoy not having all of the restrictions that they might find in their home countries. While Europe has pockets of disgruntled immigrants who try to live under *Sharia* in their neighborhoods, that has not been a problem in the United States where Muslims are more accepted by society and prosper economically. This is something all Americans should be proud of, and this should reduce our fear of Muslims in the United States.

Furthermore, the adoption of a more unified Islamic code to rule the Islamic world throughout its history did not always lead to backward-thinking or constant violence. Today we simplistically associate *Sharia* with one form of the law and with groups like the Taliban—primitive, violent, and constantly reigning in freedoms. There were long stretches of time in the Islamic world of innovation, peace, and thoughtful, theological complexity. Islamic civilization could not have become so successful had it been as unsophisticated as the faith of the Taliban or ISIS. In order for Islam to flourish, it required a law that would establish fair courts, systems of just governance, and ways of dealing with non-believers. The thousand-plus-year history of Islam has not been one of simply agreeing "*Allah* is God and everyone who doesn't believe should be killed," followed by non-stop murder and pillaging. It is not so black and white, and there were many times of genuine civilizational success. While Christians may not view Islam, Buddhism, or Hinduism as the true way, it should be understood that these ancient civilizational religions have enormously complicated theologies that defy simple generalizations.

When a group like Boko Haram or ISIS claims to implement *Sharia,* they are implementing their interpretation of the law. It naturally bends toward the most extreme, intolerant version possible so as to justify their raping, looting, and enslavement. Building a successful society on rape and murder is not possible, even in Islam. Eventually, a form of order must win out to prevent anarchy, and for most of Islamic history, *Sharia* has provided that order. Because there is no Pope or ultimate authority in Islam, *Sharia* can be interpreted many ways. There are many who live under some form of austere *Sharia* and hold to a fundamentalism that advocates for literalism, extremely modest dress for women, sexism, suspicions of all things modern, and harsh criminal punishments, such as in Saudi Arabia where stonings and beheadings are common place. But not all Islamic societies follow the same form of *Sharia*. Other nations in the Islamic world are bent more toward a Western-style of law. Others, such as some tribes in Africa, may be Muslims, but live completely according to their local tribal law. While still others ignore *Sharia* completely, as do many Muslims in the United States who are quite secularized or committed to liberal democracy. And it is certainly not the case that all fundamentalist Muslims practice *Sharia* and choose to be political and violent. Many fundamentalist Muslims believe that the affairs of this world must be left up to *Allah,* even though they are not happy with what they see in the modern world.

Jihad

Jihad is also a key part of the Islamic faith. Its definition is complex and does not necessarily mean a violent fight. That is one interpretation, and one that militant Muslims certainly adhere to in their interpretation of the faith. *Jihad* means "struggle" and is not found in the *Quran.* It is a doctrine that developed later in the history of Islam, sanctioning holy war defensively and/or offensively when Islam finds itself threatened by nonbelievers. Some present-day Muslims will argue for and adhere to an interpretation that the struggle is simply to live a good life—not to conquer or partake in violence or war. Others have waged *jihad* for specific local causes or territorial disputes. Scholars will suggest that there are different forms of Islam, while militants will argue that there should be constant war against non-Muslims until they surrender or are eradicated. As is true with so much in Islam, many schools of thought developed over time, and the one that gets the most attention is the most violent interpretation of *jihad.* What is true, however, is that there is no widespread Islamic doctrine of pacifism, even though there are Muslims who practice pacifism.

The Five Pillars of Islam

In the same way that Christianity has great diversity between Roman Catholics, Eastern Orthodox, Lutherans, Evangelicals, Pentecostals, and many other strands and branches of the faith, so does Islam. We have spoken about the diversity in Chapter 1, but it is important to note that Islam is just as capable of having variations

in its practice as Christianity. There are some major commonalities, however. Muslims believe in *Allah*, that Muhammad is the messenger of *Allah*, and that the *Quran* is *Allah's* message. There are some very key requirements for Muslims and these are known as the Five Pillars of Islam. They are as follows:

1) Shahada is the declaration that "There is no god but *Allah*, and Muhammad is his Prophet." *Shia* add to this that "Ali is the friend of God."

2) Salat is worship or prayer in which the Muslim bows in a formal, prescribed way. For *Sunni* Muslims it is required five times per day (dawn, noon, mid-afternoon, sunset, and evening). Some ritual cleaning (ablutions) may need to be done to purify oneself for the prayer time. The worshiper must pray in the direction of the *Kabah* in Mecca. A prayer rug is often used. The community worship time is at noon on Fridays and usually involves a sermon by an *Imam* or prayer leader. Men are separated from women for the worship time.

3) Zakat is a compulsory alms-giving that may include giving money, metals, merchandise used in trade, livestock, or crops given to the needy. Personal possessions cannot be used to give alms.

4) Sawm is the fast during the holy month of *Ramadan*, which is based on the ninth month of the lunar calendar. The fast begins at dawn and ends at sunset and requires abstaining from eating, drinking, smoking, and sex. In many countries, families gather and eat together at sunset and celebrate well into the night. Sometimes a predawn meal is served. It is considered good to read the entirety of the *Quran* during this month since tradition teaches that the *Quran* came down on the 27th day of Ramadan, also known as "the Night of Power."

5) The Hajj is a pilgrimage to Mecca that is required of every able bodied Muslim at least once in their lifetime. One who has accomplished this task is known as a *Hajji*. The *Hajj* takes place during the last ten days of the twelfth lunar month, and two million people from around the world attend the event annually. It is up to the Saudi Arabian government to coordinate the event and limit the number of entries per year. It is one of the most spectacular religious events in the world, with hoards of people circling the *Kabah* in the Grand Mosque in a ritual known as *Tawaf.* Other rituals include but are not limited to throwing stones at the devil and sacrificing an animal. The crowds are so enormous at the *Hajj* that it is not unheard of for people to die after being crushed.

While most Muslims around the world read the *Quran*, revere the *Haddith*, and practice the five pillars peacefully, there are small terrorist groups and movements within Islam that are violent. There are others that practice an austere from of Sharia. In many places, despite not adhering to these extremes, a very low tolerance is held for anything outside of Islamic modes of thought and conduct. The teachings of these various sources and the way they are completely wrapped up in ethnic, tribal, and familial identity make relations between Christians and Muslims strained in many places and conversions few and far between.

Discussion Questions

1. Is it surprising to read that the *Quran* honors many Christian and Jewish ideas? Why was this the case?

2. What does the author mean by suggesting that Christianity is a more global religion? How does the Bible transmit itself more cross-culturally than the *Quran?*

3. What would be the downside of Christians only being permitted to read the Bible in Aramaic?

4. How do Christians justify the violent scriptures in the Bible? How does this differ from Muslims? Are there any ways in which we may appear hypocritical from a Muslim point of view?

5. How does *Sharia* actually bring diversity to Islam?

6. What is your response to the five pillars? Are there any particular pillars that stand out to you?

The Challenge of Reaching Muslims

Unfortunately, the chance of a reader of this book ever converting a Muslim to Christianity is extremely small. There are very good reasons for this, which we will explore below. But, we should not give up hope because many Muslims are coming to Christ each day, just not always as we expect. The purpose of this chapter is not to give an overview of how to convert a Muslim. There are books and even programs and mission-agencies that specialize in that task. Instead, we will focus on why it is difficult to reach Muslims and why there are still conversions happening nonetheless.

Having Your World Undone by Conversion

To begin with, a couple of simple question for the reader: "What are the chances of you ever converting to Mormonism in this lifetime?" "What are the chances of you converting to Hinduism, which would require not just abandoning the Trinity and your form of orthodox Christianity, but the entire Christian worldview?" My guess is that for the Christian reader of this book, the chances are very small that he or she would convert. Why would it be difficult to convert to Mormonism? Here are some possible reasons:

- It is not the form of Christianity that you view as orthodox.
- It is not the faith that has brought you comfort.
- It would mean leaving your church, possibly losing friends.
- It has a different view of the Trinity.
- You are uncomfortable with the secret temple rituals.

Why would converting to Hinduism be difficult?

- You would have no support system, (no other Hindus in your community).
- The American/Western worldview would need to be abandoned in favor of an Eastern view.
- You feel a belief in Hinduism is really something for Indians.
- You would need to change your diet.
- The rest of your Christian family views it as a pagan religion, a cult, Satanic, and so forth.

As difficult as it would be for an American evangelical Christian (with our very strong opinions about orthodoxy and absolutism) to convert to Hinduism, it is even more difficult for most Muslims to convert to Christianity.

To begin with, many Muslims grow up in societies and cultures where everyone is born a Muslim. It is a cultural, historical, familial, tribal designation—not simply a religion. It is only in the past couple centuries (mainly in the West), that religion has become something that is apart from one's culture, family, and civilization. Westerners are unusual in that they view religion as an aspect of their lives that they can freely choose to take part or reject. Most Muslims (and most human beings throughout history) have not grown up with such an individualistic mindset that relegates religion to something other than your whole life and identity.

Furthermore, having religion completely dominate your national, ethnic, familial, and societal identity means there really is no daily life beyond the religion. It is nearly impossible to separate Russian culture from its history of Russian Orthodoxy or Catholicism from a Polish person, which is why it should be no surprise that Evangelical Christianity barely grows in either of those places. Rituals, festivals, holidays, names, and many other factors of daily society are deeply ingrained in the religious faith of these nations. This is even more the case in Muslim nations. In the case of Pakistan and Bangladesh, they were carved away from India to create a Muslim nation, separate from the Hindu-dominated Indian nation. There may be increased secularism, but a total conversion to a faith from a different civilization is very rare.

Another issue is that the blowback may be severe. It may be that by converting to a foreign faith, your family will disown you, you may never get a job in your country, you may never find someone to marry, or your children may be taken from you. In the Islamic world it can often mean that you will be killed for dishonoring your family. Jesus' words about "hating your mother and father" (Luke 14:26) makes more sense in this context, in that to follow Jesus was truly to break with the world and civilization that you once knew—and your family may be the ones who punish you the most.

Another issue is that many Muslims have never heard the gospel preached, but they have seen Western "Christian" culture, including American culture, and they find it decadent and hypocritical. How can a "Christian nation" allow women to dress as they do, make pornographic movies, raise children who do not respect their elders, and go to war all the time? Of course the answer is that Western society is not really dominated by Christian values. It has Christian, ancient Roman, ancient Greek, and secular humanistic values undergirding it. For Muslims, that separation between our society and religion should not exist. So our Western problems are seen as a problem with our religion or evidence of our lack of religion. Christian fundamentalists feel much the same way! Since there may not be many Christians in the area where a Muslim lives, they belong to a rival tribe, or they only know Christianity from what they see happening in the West—the prejudice is enormous. Most Muslims are not impressed with the piety of Christians, who can't even find the resolve to pray to God five times a day.

Furthermore, when your nation or tribe has been invaded by people of a particular faith (as is the case for many Muslim nations), it becomes hard to be open to the people of that religion—no matter what they say. In the same way that many Americans find Muslims telling us that "September 11 was not about Islam," most Muslims find it hollow to suggest that Western colonialism, imperialism, or other incursions in the Muslim world are not linked to Christianity.

Finally, many Muslims live in countries where Christianity is illegal or missionary proselytizing is not allowed and can be deadly. Few Christians (usually from very different civilizations and worldviews) manage to gain proximity to Muslim communities. And once the Christian evangelists are there, it can take a lot of time to gain trust and build relationships, and it all must be done underground or in secret. It is a time-consuming, discouraging, and often dangerous process that usually does not yield large numbers of converts.

One of the ironies of the post-September 11 world is that Americans and Europeans do not want Muslims moving to their countries and trying to convert people, yet Western Christians have increased their efforts to do this in Muslim lands, usually breaking local laws. We do it because we claim it is "God's will" and part of the "Great Commission;" however, this is the way Muslims feel as well, believing that it is their divine duty to spread Islam.

How Does Conversion Happen in the Islamic World?

The good news is that many Muslims are converting to Christianity. It is rarely because Westerners have memorized Christian systematic theology and can out-debate a Muslim on theological points. Those kinds of apologetics are rooted in a more Western, post-Enlightenment form of thinking, which downplays revelation and the mystical elements in our world in favor of a more systematic, rational way of explaining spiritual issues. This does not play well in much of the Islamic world, and it doesn't even play well in much of the Christian world outside of the United States and Western Europe. Once again, we Western Christians tend to value "facts" and a "scientific approach" more than most Muslims, Christians, Buddhists, and Hindus. For most of them, the world is very much alive with the mystical, mysterious, and unexplainable, and their faith encounters may happen every day. It is ironic that so many evangelicals place so much emphasis on their ability to create modern techniques and "rational discourse" on theology that will convert Muslims. This often misses not only the point, but also the entire worldview as well!

Instead, Muslims are more likely to be coming to Christ because they are having dreams, visions, or suffering persecution; not because they are reading Josh McDowell's book *More than a Carpenter*. In some cases, they are seeing supernatural miracles occur. There are many instances of Muslims being fascinated with Jesus as he is found in the *Quran* and they ask Jesus to appear to them, and he does! Others cry out to God for the truth and Christ appears to them in dreams and visions.

Amazing News from the Islamic World

If all of the news out of the Islamic world seems discouraging, have hope! God is at work! While it is true that Islam is in a dangerous phase, that Christians are being persecuted, and it is still difficult for us to convert Muslims, God is doing something amazing and it is not being reported on in the news (which is perhaps a good thing). Amidst all the turmoil occurring, Christian revivals are breaking out in the Islamic world.

In all of the nearly fourteen-hundred-year history of Islam, there have only been 13 movements of Muslim communities turning to

Christ.[6] That is a remarkably small number. But here is the most amazing statistic: since the 21st century began and in the aftermath of September 11, 2001, there have been an additional 69 movements to Christ.[7] This is simply astonishing!

David Garrison, who traveled 250,000 miles and conducted more than one thousand interviews in the Islamic world, tracked these movements over two and a half years. He divided the regions experiencing movements into "Nine Geo Cultural Rooms": 1) West Africa, 2) North Africa, 3) East Africa, 4) The Arab World, 5) The Persian World, 6) Turkestan, 7) Western South Asia, 8) Eastern South Asia, and 9) Indo-Malaysia.[8]

Why Are Muslims Converting to Christianity?

The speed at which these movements are growing is exciting, unusual, and encouraging. Why is this happening? Is it a sign that the end of the world is near? Not necessarily. While 69 new movements have emerged since the year 2000, it is still a small number compared to the one and half billion Muslims in the world. Furthermore, both Islam and Christianity are getting a much wider audience because of the Internet. Youtube is a place where anyone can get religious preaching at any time of day. Old ideas can be challenged by exposure to the Internet and globalization, but it can also reaffirm ancient ideas, creeds, and beliefs. The Internet also empowers the more radical elements of Islam. But since September 11, 2001, the Islamic world has also started to be exposed and awakened to a lot of its ancient, unresolved problems. This and other issues help to explain this sudden growth of Christian movements. Let us look at some of the reasons Muslims are turning to Christianity like never before:

---

6. David Garrison, *A Wind in the House of Islam: How God is Drawing Muslims Around the Word to Faith in Jesus Christ.* (Monument: WIGTake Resources.), Loc. 325, Kindle version.

7. Ibid.

8. Ibid., Loc. 368, Kindle version.

Disillusionment with Militant Islam

One of the effects of the rise of Al-Qaeda, ISIS, and other Islamic militant groups is a growing disillusionment with Islam. Disgusted with or embarrassed by attacks on innocents, the brutal savagery of the militants, the perpetual divisions within Islam, or as a result of undergoing personal persecution, there are significant numbers of Muslims who are turning to secularism or Christianity. Underground Christian movements exist throughout the Islamic world, and through radio, podcasts, Youtube, underground missionaries, and aid workers, Muslims are getting the gospel message and turning to Christ.

For instance, the refugee camps in Jordan that have grown because of the Syrian War are so large, they now make up the second largest city in the whole country. Churches grow in these tent cities as people learn that there is a better path. This new faith has an emphasis on a personal God, who cares about His people and offers forgiveness and healing as opposed to expectations that are ritual-based or a demand to hate one's neighbor. Hating one's neighbor is exhausting and a perpetual state of fury is not easy to keep up nor is it healthy. The intimacy and peace of the Christian faith is a stark contrast to the Islamic faith that they know. It brings the refugees a deep sense of peace.

The fact that groups like ISIS are constantly quoting the *Quran* actually opens hearts to the Bible and starts to discredit the *Quran*. If the Muslims are quoting the *Quran* while they kill their friends, family, and neighbors, tremendous questions are raised in their minds about this supposed "holy book." Suddenly, comparing and the *Quran* with the words of Christ in the New Testament has become very appealing and relevant.

Disillusionment with Islamic Governments

Underground Christianity is flourishing in Iran. Iran has a long history as a civilization separate from the Arab world and was always a nation quite liberal in its values and very committed to the passions of this life. The Islamic Revolution of 1979, with its austere form of Islam, was an aberration in the country, and *Shia* Islam was imposed on the whole country. The theocracy (a combination of religion and politics as a governmental system) in Iran has been a disaster for the Islamic faith there. People in Iran now associate Islam with corrupt religious leaders, bad government, and oppression. This is particularly the case among Iranian youth who love the West, love the United States, and are desperate to be free of Islamic theocracy. Iran has been living out in practice what Osama bin Laden and ISIS preach, and the result has been a wrecked economy and society as well as widespread disillusionment with Islam.

Today Iran is a nation where there is a tremendous party scene, widespread drug addiction, prostitution, secularism, and a movement that wants true democracy and freedom. The great Islamic revolution has been a total disaster. The "Green Revolution" was a 2009 uprising that sought to overthrow the Islamic regime. Although it failed, it exposed how widespread the discontent with the government in Iran is, and how cynical Iranians have become about the Islamic faith and its religious leaders. All of this disillusionment has meant that hearts in Iran are more open to Christianity than ever before. Churches must remain underground, but Iran is a place where many are turning to Christ and the Lord is at work building His church.

Contextualizing the Gospel

In the troubled areas of the Arab world, many Christians will share about the figures they revere in the Bible, such as Abraham, in order to connect with Muslims. "Why was Abraham willing to sacrifice his son Isaac?" and "Why was the sacrifice not required?" Contrasting the roles of blood, sacrifice, and ritual in the Old Testament with the deeper interpretations of those aspects of the faith fulfilled through Jesus in the New Testament speaks their language. The process is one of using familiar language, people, and symbols to juxtapose how Islam is more rooted in the ritualistic, graceless faith of the pagan era and falls short of the grace-filled, forgiveness-based salvation of Christianity. The approach must be about building on the narrative they know, as opposed to introducing aspects of the Christian faith that are more relevant and important to Western Christians. There are some groups, often led by former Muslims or Christians from the Middle East with negative views of Islam that try a more combative, rational approach, but the greatest weapon of all is the gentle love of Christ.

Somewhat controversial is the fact that Islam is also growing among those who do not fully abandon their Islamic ways, but accept Christ as their savior. The large Christian conversion in Bangladesh among the Muslim Salet people is an example of a contextualization that does not totally jettison everything about Islam. Mosques are retained much in the same way that Paul continued to preach in the synagogue. The name for Jesus is interpreted into the Arabic *"Issa,"* the way we use "Jesus" in English as opposed to how his name would have been spelled or pronounced in Aramaic. Even the pilgrimage and prostrating oneself five times a day is kept, although that is done toward Jerusalem instead of Mecca (as Muhammad originally had done it before his broken relationship with the Jews). As long as there is no contradiction to Scripture, Islamic traditions can be kept although processed in a Christian way and for a Christian purpose. Not wearing shoes in the mosque is retained as "the followers of *Issa*" pray to Jesus Christ. This should not be a big issue for Western Christians. In addition there are other traditions Muslims have that actually enhance the Christian life—such as the way that mosques are open at all times, maintaining a place of constant fellowship, as opposed to Christian churches, which are often closed and unused for much of the week, something Muslims find unusual and not very community-based. (Mosques serve somewhat as a community court-yard where people hang out whether there is any activity going on or not.) Worship may also be on Friday instead of Sunday, although many Evangelical churches have services on Saturdays as well as Sundays.

Even the word "Christian" might be eliminated because it conjures up the image of a hypocritical Westerner or of Christian imperial-ism. Using the term "followers of *Issa*" is similar to the way many missional churches in the West now use the term "Christ-follower" instead of Christian, fearing that the word "Christian" is too vague, is too institutional, or has too much cultural and historical baggage.

Inevitably, local culture always sifts into our Christian expres-sions. This is something all Christians have to be on guard against. We must always allow Scripture to critique our cultures. "Chrislam" is controversial in that some fear it goes too far trying to fit in with Islam to convert people to Christianity. The arguments, however, are nuanced, and we should not underestimate how often in Christian history this form of contextualization has led to strong, orthodox Christian movements. It is always important to remember that what makes Christianity more global than Islam is that the New Testament made the faith easy to be contextualized by all nations—as opposed to being rooted in some particularly holy culture and place like Arabia or Israel. We do not want to limit the ways Muslims adapt to Christianity when that is clearly what happened constantly throughout the New Testament as the Christian faith spread beyond the Jews of Jerusalem.

The Power of God's Revelation

Throughout the Islamic world, Muslims report seeing visions of Jesus, or hearing Jesus speak directly to them after they meditate on the question of "Who is Jesus?" in the *Quran*. The fact that the *Quran* respects Jesus plants a curiosity in many Muslims about this historical figure they are to revere, and Christ makes himself known to those searching for him. Divine encounters with Jesus occur constantly in the Islamic world.

It is important to remember that Muslims in a debate are not likely to ever agree with a Christian trying to convert them about certain aspects of the Christian faith such as the Trinity. Many Muslims come from a face-based culture where to lose an argument is dishonorable. When those big theological shifts happen they tend to happen as a result of personal revelation or an encounter with Scripture on their own time. Others convert during a time of crisis or after watching a Christian for a long period of time and noticing that the Christian behaves differently and has a peace that Muslims do not possess. A quick conversion is unlikely, and it will most likely involve much more than mere words or debates. Most Muslims are not requesting a rational explanation such as Sam Harris, the late Christopher Hitchens, or Richard Dawkins have asked for in their writing and debates with Christians. They are asking for a new revelation that replaces their old revelation. Ironically, Muslims have a view of the spiritual world that is more tangible and present everyday than many Western Christians. This is one of the reasons our Christian faith can seem so "dead" to Muslims. It looks as if it is a compartmentalized part of our life, while Islam teaches that the physical and the spiritual are all one. Western Christians often fail to realize that our spiritual lives are not that integrated into our daily lives in comparison to Muslims and a lot of non-Western Christians.

The average Western evangelical Christian, for instance, does not put much stock into their dreams, but the Bible takes dreams seriously and so do Muslims. Fortunately, God does, too, and Christ is making himself known to Muslims.

Translation of the Bible

Unlike the *Quran*, which must be in classical Arabic, the Bible is meant to be translated into all languages. No one language or culture holds a monopoly on God's Word. This means that the Bible is being translated into the languages of the Islamic world. In many cases, Muslims throughout history have never had access to any holy book in their own language—neither the Quran nor the Bible. This is an important point to remember when we think of how few Muslims have converted over the years. A goat-herder in Afghanistan, a tribal chief in the Sahara, or a fisherman on a remote Indonesian island may be illiterate, unable to read or speak Arabic, and may have learned about Islam only through what he and his family have been told for generations. The *Quran* has remained out of reach for many Muslims for many centuries. Christians may never have been present, neither would there have been Christian Scriptures in their obscure languages. But all of that is changing rapidly, and it gives Christianity an advantage. Once translated, the reader has the right to receive divine revelation directly from God. They need not learn Arabic or wait for some holy man to tell them what to believe; the Word belongs to them. This is revolutionary and unusual for millions of Muslims.

Furthermore, when the spiritual terms begin to have the local language of the people, the people have a much deeper contact with the divine because the message of God is in their "heart language." There is simply no substitute for having God's Word in the language you dream in, communicate with, and think with daily. The Bible translated is immensely important, and it touches people in a way that the Arabic *Quran* cannot.

As Lamin Sanneh of Yale University has noted in his scholarly work throughout the years, having the Word of God in one's own language empowers the local culture and frees it from being oppressed from the outside. There is a sense of ownership that empowers local culture, instead of robbing it of its uniqueness. Islam, on the other hand, very much imposes Arabic culture and values on the societies it touches, which is why sometimes an Indonesian Muslim woman is dressed like a woman from the sands of Arabia.

Comparing Jesus and Muhammad

Last, as we have mentioned, the figure of Jesus is very enticing. Unlike Muhammad, he never made war on anyone, he did not have multiple wives (Muhammad's wives included a pre-pubescent child), his words transmit peace, and the stories of his life transmit a grace that is foreign in Islam. The incarnation and the forgiveness of sins that comes with Christ's resurrection are things not found in Islam, which relegates both Jesus and Muhammad to the role of human prophet. Perhaps nothing is more compelling than Jesus' continual promise to forgive sins and guarantee paradise to his followers. The fact that one can truly know that one's sins are forgiven is something that eludes many Muslims and creates tension, fear, and a sense of perpetual condemnation in their spiritual lives.

Why Westerners Do Not Do Well Converting Muslims

It is unusual for a Western Christian to convert a Muslim. Much of the conversion that is taking place is happening because of Jesus appearing to Muslims, persecution, and a sense of dissatisfaction with what is happening in the Islamic world. Furthermore, to become a Christian is often to leave one's family, daily traditions, culture, and entire worldview. It is not as easy as it is for many Westerners who grow up thinking of religion as an optional, individualistic, private matter. Here are some further reasons why Westerners are not always effective at converting Muslims:

Not Willing to Enter into a Deep Relationship

The saying that "no one cares how much you know, until they know how much you care," is an apt one for any missionary or evangelist. Many Westerners want to preach the gospel once and expect an immediate response or conversion. With Muslims, the decision to leave the faith is enormous (as it would be for us as Christians). Befriending a Muslim simply to convert them and failing to develop a deep relationship is not a good idea. Muslims should not be viewed as a commodity, nor should we view ourselves as the Messiah figures saving them from hell. The Christian command is to love, and we do this by developing long-term, no-strings-attached relationships. Most likely, a Christian who begins a friendship with a Muslim will find many things in common: a concern for sin in society, conservative values, and a belief that the spiritual world matters daily. Remember, very few Muslims are out to hurt or attack Western Christians. Like most evangelicals, they simply wish we would convert to their faith.

Rational Approach

Another common mistake is getting into debates on systematic theology. The reality is that both Islam and Christianity have beliefs that are not necessarily provable, rational, or possible to explain. Paul said that the message of the cross is "foolishness to those who are perishing, but to us who are being saved it is the power of God" (1 Corinthians 1:18). Many Muslims can argue against Christianity very well. One of the biggest problems they have with Christianity is its "polytheism" because of our belief in the Trinity. The Trinity is never really easy for any Christian to explain—if we are honest—and it is not doctrine that saves Muslims. Rather it is an encounter with the resurrected, living Christ who has the power to forgive sins. Excessive amounts of back-and-forth debate are not likely to lead to conversion. Living a different kind of life as a Christian and showing compassion and love is a better approach. One of the best things a Christian can do for a Muslim friend is to say, "I am praying for you." They value the spiritual and are touched that we care about them and believe that the great God will listen to your prayers specifically for them.

The Need to Demonize Islamic Peoples

As Christians we do not believe that Islam is the way, that the *Quran* has a divine message, or that Muhammad was God's prophet. But we absolutely must believe that Christ died for *all* sinners and "God wants all people to be saved and to come to a knowledge of the truth" (1 Timothy 2:4). Islamic civilization has given the world algebra, the compass, great poetry, literature, Islamic art, chemistry, geology, spherical trigonometry, and, for a period of time, was far more advanced than Western Christian civilization. It did not always struggle with the anti-intellectualism and discomfort with pluralism that it does now. Furthermore, as we have seen throughout this book, there are many Muslims who are marginal in their faith or more committed to their local culture than to Islam. We cannot simply demonize them all as if they are all card-carrying members of *Al-Qaeda*. Demonizing non-Christians is a way of distancing ourselves from them and not having to do the hard work of getting to know them and loving them. It is far easier to label them all as hopeless and walk away or live in perpetual anger and fear. Listening to the media encourages viewing the issues in the Islamic world in the most simplistic, dualistic light and encourages constant fear. Instead we should be educating ourselves and praying for those who wish to do us harm, as many Christians who are actually persecuted do in the Middle East.

Malala Yousafzai was a fourteen-year-old girl who spoke three languages and lived in the dangerous Swat Valley in Pakistan where the Taliban was increasingly gaining influence. Asked by the BBC to blog about her life as a young schoolgirl, she became a target for the Taliban, who are against the education of women and had been burning down schools. On October 9, 2012, while on her bus returning from school, Malala was shot in the head by a Taliban gunman. Upon recovering, Malala, a practicing Muslim, responded by saying that she wished the man, who had disfigured her face permanently, no harm and had forgiven him in her heart. If this is what a young Muslim girl can do after being shot in the face, why do so many Christians in the West, refuse to pray or care about Muslims?

The Challenge of Life after Conversion

Those we must uphold in prayer the most are the converts to Christianity from Islam. Muslim background believers are not only hated, disowned, and often killed for their faith in Jesus, they are also often viewed with great skepticism by other Christians who fear they are just there to infiltrate the Christian church. Christians may reject new Muslim believers because they fear attacks or simply do not trust them. Others may be suspicious of new converts traveling alone without a family. Could they be terrorists? In many cases, they are Christian converts who have lost everything. Some may never have the opportunity to return to their homeland or have a job again. They may want to immigrate to a "Christian" country like the United States, but may be shocked to find that the Christian people in the United States are against letting them into their country— even when they are Christians fleeing persecution!

In the coming years, there may be many women, children, and others who seek refuge in the United States and other Western countries. Some of these will be people who have suffered tremendously due to violence done in the name of Islam. Others may be Christian minorities, recent converts, or immigrants who are seriously open to Christianity. What will the response of the Western church be to these refugees and immigrants from an Islamic background? Will we choose anger and self-protection? Or will we view this as yet another opportunity in the work God is doing through the events in the Islamic world?

Discussion Questions:

1. Would you be willing to convert to Mormonism, Hinduism, Islam, or another faith? Why or why not? What kind of approach would someone have to have to convert you away from Christianity?

2. Why is it difficult for a Muslim to convert?

3. What are some problems or hypocritical aspects that Muslims might identify regarding Christianity and Western society?

4. Do you think you have what it takes to be a missionary to the Islamic world? Why or Why not?

5. How would you react to a large community of Syrian or Iraqi refugees settling in your hometown?

6. Does the challenge Muslim converts face seem eye-opening to you? Read the account of Saul's conversion in Acts 9. Does the information in this chapter bring new light to this story?

Chapter 5

Islam, Violence, and Territorial Expansion

Does Islam have a problem with violence? The short, but politically-incorrect answer is "yes." In comparison to other religions, there is a disproportionate amount of violence today both within Islam and between Islam and other faiths. While every religion has its fundamentalists and violent militants (and they are always a minority, including in Islam today), there are some unique characteristics of Islam that lend themselves toward a more consistent level of militancy. We will explore those in this chapter. But first, we must look at the objections Muslims and other apologists for the Islamic faith will make, if it is claimed that Islam has a tendency toward violence.

Objections to Islam Being Labeled a Religion of Violence

Objection 1:

Islam is no more violent than other religions.

The level of violence in all religions is often dramatically overestimated. A recent survey shows only 4 percent of conflicts historically had to do with religion. Most wars have to do with land, resources, tribal conflict, ancient feuds, and other things outside of religion. That is the case with Islam; it is rarely only about religion.

Furthermore, we can see violence within all religions from time to time. There are militant Jews who act violently in Israel, Buddhist orders that have acted violently against other Buddhist orders, and Christians who have butchered Christians in Rwanda.

OBJECTION 2:

Christianity has a violent past and has other ways to make violence legitimate.

The Crusades and the Inquisition are an example of Christian violence. "Christian kings" and "Christian armies" descended on Muslim lands to take back Jerusalem. Furthermore, Europe saw hundreds of years of religious violence, consisting primarily of Christians fighting Christians (Protestant versus Catholic and other sectarian warfare). In addition "Christian nations" and empires subjugated Muslim peoples throughout Europe and the Middle East, carved out new borders in ancient tribal lands, and colonized Islamic countries. Finally, there are other ways Christians can be violent: supporting the military, bombings, or drone strikes of their "Christian nation," as the United States does with its presidents who claim to be Christian.

OBJECTION 3:

The violence we see has to do with cultural factors, Western imperialism, and ethnic tribalism—not Islam.

In general, the violence we see in the Islamic world is the result of many historical, cultural, and political factors and is not necessarily about Islam. Western-supported authoritarianism, colonialism, and the end of the Cold War created havoc in the Middle East and Central Asia. This has greatly impacted the region, leading to violent movements and uprisings to bring justice.

OBJECTION 4:

While the Quran teaches peace, there is no control over how it is interpreted.

There are many *surahs* that teach peace and tolerance toward non-Muslims such as "no compulsion in religion," and *Surah* 16:125 says that arguing with unbelievers should be done in "ways that are best and most gracious." And there are many Scriptures in the Old

Testament that preach violence. Why should Christians get to pick and choose which verses are still relevant, but Muslims cannot?

OBJECTION 5:

Islam has a long history of peacefully co-existing with its neighbors.

The militant side of Islam is mostly a new occurrence and throughout Islamic history, Islamic civilization was often more tolerant of religious minorities than Christian empires were, granting freedom of religion, for instance.

An Informed Christian Response

These five objections all have points to consider and some are based in fact, but they are not very nuanced. It is true that religious violence (Christian or Muslim) is often highly exaggerated and most wars are about things other than theological differences. And yes, Christianity does have a bloody history that stretches from the ferocious battles between Catholics and Protestants in Europe to the violent church-sanctioned colonization of Latin America and the Atlantic slave trade. Even in today's world, the sight of Christians fighting Christians in the Rwandan massacre was a sign that these incidents did not just happen in the past. Furthermore, a lot of terrorism is fueled by ancient grievances over land and conquest. Not only did Western "Christian nations" like France, Britain, and the United States meddle and interfere in Islamic lands, but so did Eastern "Christian nations" such as Russia, which turned many Central Asian, predominantly Islamic nations into Soviet satellites. These historical incursions become about national oppression more than they are about Islam versus Christianity.

Also, it is true that there were times in history when the Islamic civilization was more respectful of people of other faiths (and even the philosophies and ideas of other civilizations) than were Christian lands. There are many Muslims who genuinely believe that Islam is a religion of peace. There are enough words of tolerance in the *Quran* for them to justify that statement, whether we agree or not.

These points have to be dealt with, and they do explain a lot of the violence that has been done in the name of Islam. Both Christianity and Islam have had a long history of people committing violence in the name of their founder and both are absolutist religions that are not truly open to considering other paths to truth. This makes them very easy to exploit and militarize. Additionally, they both aggressively try to convert each other.

Conceding these points, however, does not tell the whole story. Muhammad is the only leader of a major religion who used force to try to establish a religious, social, and political order in the *immediate* world. From its inception, Islam had an aggressive, missionary zeal. Christianity and Buddhism also have had a strong missionary emphasis, but neither of those faiths started from a position of power. Muhammad's military campaigns immediately won him territory and overturned Arab society right out of the gate. A new political, religious ideology was introduced that undid the ancient tribal systems and demanded loyalty. From the beginning, Islam went to war and was victorious. While the *Quran* itself does not say to kill people unless they convert, it does clearly justify fighting and giving people a choice between, conversion, submission, paying taxes, or continuing in battle.[9] Many *Haddith* as well as future Islamic leaders were even more forceful.[10] Early Muslims glorify war as their pre-Islamic ancestors did. The Constitution of Medina also makes it clear that there is a separation between the converted and non-converted that must be bridged through militancy. Muhammad in his farewell address said to "fight all men until they say there is no God but Allah"[11]

---

9. Hugh Kennedy, *The Great Arab Conquests: How the Spread of Islam Changed the World We Live In* (Philadelphia: Da Capo Press), 50.

10. Efraim Karsh, *Islamic Imperialism: A History* (New Haven: Yale University Press, 2013).

11. Ibid.

Christianity, on the other hand, spent three hundred years as a minority faith that was persecuted by the Roman Empire. It is fair to say that the DNA of Christianity and Islam was set in the early years of the movement. For Christianity, the movement would be tempted with ideas of power and conquest, but the DNA would always be uneasy with efforts to make the faith about conquest and empire over servant hood. Islam, however, has a DNA that was shaped by conquering this current world immediately by force. Purification was by force, and meant to be total. This contrasts greatly with Jesus who ended up crucified and with disciples who ran away. His Kingdom was clearly not of this world.

The Islamic Need for Territorial Expansionism

As we have already seen, Islam was born in Arabia amidst a culture of regular warfare, vendettas, and fragile alliances between the many tribes at this important crossroad of global trade. Arab culture and religion was primitive in comparison to the more sophisticated empires that had existed in the region (Rome, Byzantium, Persia, Egypt, Assyria, Babylon) and monotheistic faiths like Christianity and Judaism had sacred Scriptures and advanced theologies that surpassed the simple superstitions of the Arab peoples. Muhammad was a political and military leader who called people to a more complicated, pure monotheism. He believed that God had led him to "fight all men until they say, "There is no god, but Allah." *Quran* 9:5 says, "When the sacred months are past, kill the idolaters wherever you find them, and seize them, besiege them and lie in wait for them in every place of ambush; but if they repent, pray regularly, and give the alms tax, then let them go their way, for God is forgiving, merciful."

While Jesus Christ made a clear distinction between God and Caesar and said the kingdom of God was not of this world, Muhammad felt an immediate need to bring monotheism, justice, and a new order to Arabia and beyond. He did that through warfare. Christianity also went through a painful process of fusing religion and politics, which led to religious wars, the Crusades, the wars of religion, colonialism, and many other tragedies. This was a deviation from its founding ideas—not a direct result of those basic ideas. The Crusades are often brought up by Muslims and secular people alike, but are often misunderstood.[12] All of these things required a massive twisting and mischaracterization of the words and nature of Jesus of Nazareth. Furthermore, those ideas were eventually critiqued from *within* Christianity. Christianity, unlike Islam, had a reformation.

Adult male Bedouins of Arabia were raised as warriors from birth, unlike the disciples in Palestine.[13] For Muhammad and Islam, the world is divided into *Dar al-Islam* (The House of Islam) where Islamic rule dominates and *Dar al-Harb*, the rest of the world that is inhabited by non-Muslims and led by infidels. When Muhammad was chased out of Mecca by unbelievers; he found allies in *Yathrib* (Medina) and founded a movement not based on tribes and blood-lines, but on these ideas of a new, pure faith. This new religious movement went from being a marginal religion within the state to actually becoming the state.[14]

Both Jesus and Muhammad upset the local religious and political orders. In Jesus' case, he told his disciples to put away their swords and ended up on the cross. In Muhammad's case, he went to war and won. The fact that Muhammad won rather easily and Islam expanded territorially very quickly, led to a very interesting founda-tional dilemma for Islam that would forever affect its DNA. Islam was almost instantaneously turning into an empire, thus creating a need for constant territorial expansion.

---

12. http://www.firstthings.com/article/2009/06/inventing-the-crusades

13. Hugh Kennedy, *The Great Arab Conquests: How the Spread of Islam Changed the World We Live In*" (Philadelphia: Da Capo Press), 39.

14. Efraim Karsh. *Islamic Imperialism: A History*, (New Haven: Yale University Press, 2007), 13.

Efraim Karsh in his book, *Islamic Imperialism: A History*, makes the astute point that the disbanding of the old order of tribal warfare and subsistence on the raiding of caravans meant that a new order had to replace it quickly if people were to be able to make a living. As Islam expanded territorially, it suddenly had distant lands that it needed to control, manage, and maintain. And those lands had resources and wealth that the Islamic conquerors could take to keep Arabia fed. But Arab society was primitive and tribal, unlike the empires that surrounded Arabia. Consequently, "Arab bureaucratic and administrative inexperience, forced the victors to rely on the existing Byzantine and Iranian empire systems for running their nascent empire."[15] The trappings of an empire were adopted by the Muslim conquerors to sustain Arabia and manage the newly conquered lands.

Islam's comfort with an empire came much more quickly than in Christianity. Muhammad's desire for justice and piety in this world meant that the non-Muslim world was in the way of God's plan for all people. Muhammad's way of dealing with non-believers often involved force, so it can be said that Islam was started by a prophet who was a military man, who believed it was the duty of all Muslims to usher in a completely Islamic world, and who believed that a theocratic empire was the way to do it.

Muhammad initially allied himself with the Jews, impressed as he was by the stories of their sophisticated faith. But the Jews of Medina rejected him and ridiculed the inconsistencies in the *Quran* and its inaccurate description of Old Testament stories. Muhammad was also dismayed to learn that the Christians passing through Arabia not only preached the "polytheistic" Trinity (three gods in one), but that Christians rarely agreed with each other on their Christian theology. In a key moment of turning away from Christianity and

---

15. Ibid., 28.

Judaism, Muhammad changed the direction of prayer and prostration from the direction of Jerusalem to the direction of Mecca. Friday became the Sabbath, and the *muezzin* and minaret replaced Jewish trumpets and Christian bells. Islam, from that point on, would view Christianity and Judaism as inferior faiths.

Medina soon became a capital city, of sorts. Muhammad lived there and taxes were collected and decisions were made for the quickly expanding religious state. Since Islam was the one true religion, and Muhammad the final prophet, it was the duty of this theocratic state to expand this true message to the whole world. Like Christianity, Islam would be an absolutist faith: "There is only one way." But in this case, the message was coming from a state with armed men, not 12 dusty disciples.

Within 12 years of Muhammad's death, the Persian Empire was collapsing and Syria and Egypt had been taken from the Byzantine Empire. In a few short years, Muslims had conquered Central Asia, parts of Europe, and were pressing upon China and India. Not everyone was forced to become Muslim initially. The most pressing need was securing a tribute from the various conquered peoples.[16]

During the Caliphate of Umar (634-44 CE), all conquered lands became part of the Muslim community. Karsh writes: "The decision effectively extended Muhammad's designation of Islam as the cornerstone of the political order to the entire Middle East. This principle would be maintained for over a millennium until the collapse of the Ottoman Empire in the wake of World War I and the subsequent abolition of the caliphate."[17] Conquered lands would not be settled, but rather the conquerors would keep moving on in battle, forever expanding the House of Islam.

Conquered people of other faiths were given a protected community status (*Dhimmis*) in which they were allowed to practice their

16. Ibid 23.
17. Ibid, 26.

religion and keep their property. However, they were forced to pay high taxes, were subject to persecution, were not able to hold religious activities outside of their churches or synagogues, and were prohibited by punishment of death to share their faith with Muslims. Jews and Christians had to wear particular clothes that set them apart, and Muslim lords could ride horses while others could only ride donkeys.[18] Non-Arabs were often not encouraged to convert because the Islamic empire was dependent on second-class citizens doing much of the work needed for the Arabs to maintain their wealth and superior status.

While Arabs and Muslims were greatly outnumbered in their quickly expanding empire, by the eighth century, Arabic had become the official language, allowing the various conquered people to contribute to the rise of Islamic civilization, which would go on to be more advanced than European civilization for centuries.[19]

The Muslims studied mathematics, medicine, and astronomy ideas from India, politics, economics, and administration from the Persians, and botany, zoology, and philosophy from the Greeks, among many other things.[20] Furthermore, the Islamic empire was not always at war, having found it helpful to trade with many distant nations from Central Asia to Africa.

The rise of Islam was so sudden and so all-encompassing (in territory and in the arts and sciences), that it was very traumatic for the Islamic world when Europe began to rise, and the Islamic world began to decline. The loss of Islamic Spain in 1492 was so shocking that Muslims (including the late Osama Bin Laden) still speak of it. The final great Islamic empire (the Ottoman Empire) sided with Germany in World War I and eventually collapsed, forming the

---

18. Ibid, 28.
19. Ibid, 28-29.
20. Ibid, 67-68.

secular state of Turkey. The Islamic empire had been rebuked, and a new experiment with secularism was beginning in the Middle East.

A Less Flexible Faith

Much of Islam's history is full of successful territorial expansion, widespread adoption of the faith by foreign peoples, and moments of cultural, artistic, and scientific triumph. All of that historical success has left the Islamic world very nostalgic about the past. Unlike Christians who tend to be forward-looking and do not have much nostalgia for anything other than the early church, the Islamic world has many events, peoples, and battles that painfully linger in their memory—either because they long to return to that glory or are haunted by a past failure.

For a substantial amount of Islamic leaders and groups throughout history, the expanding Islamic Empire of the past is the ideal for this world. It is what Muhammad modeled for them, and what he said *Allah* wants.

Islam, like Christianity, Judaism, Buddhism, and Hinduism, has produced movements that are violent, teach hatred of non-believers, have no tolerance for heterodoxy or disagreement, and are willing to start revolutions to usher in a new religious order. All faiths produce highly intolerant sects.

However, the number of groups that will violently pursue those goals in the Christian and Jewish faiths has greatly been reduced by enlightenment ideas of reason, particularly the right for man to choose his own beliefs, as well as other concepts such as the successful separation of church and state throughout the world, the equality of women, the abolition of the death penalty, and the freedom of expression. The ideas of "modernity" (the post-Enlightenment modern world) spread throughout most countries and civilizations, but often had a hard time penetrating the Islamic world.

Other older regions of the world were always more comfortable with pluralism than the Islamic world. In Hindu and Buddhist lands, states and empires were inherently more pluralistic and diverse for longer periods of time. Choosing different gods in most of East Asia, Africa, or the Indian subcontinent is not offensive the way it is in Muslim lands. Polytheism is often part of the natural landscape in those regions.

However, for Islam, many things are off-limits. Putting the *Quran* under the kind of textual and historical scrutiny that the Bible endures, for instance, is one example. Allowing people to abandon their Islamic faith without fear of shunning, punishment, or death is another example. Allowing women complete and total freedom of their bodies and minds is another area where Islam retains many of the ideas that fit more with ancient Arabia's cultural mores than today's societies. Western customs may be decadent or unholy by Islamic or Christian standards, but there is far less freedom of choice in Islam than in other faiths to embrace standards outside of the faith.

Last, Islam's geographic center (the Arabian Peninsula and Mesopotamia) is a part of the world that is particularly divided. Unlike Africa or Latin America, which can also be plagued with civil wars and violence at times, the Arab world and Iran have a multitude of different ethnic groups, sects, tribes, and nations— all that are all very much linked to an absolutist religion's empire that has been in constant conflict since its inception. It is as if the wars of Christendom had started with Jesus and were continuing on to this day. Christian Republicanism was very much tempered by Roman and Greek thought as well as the critiques from the secular European Enlightenment. Since Christ's kingdom is not of this world, Christianity was able to enter into a dialogue with the ideas of other civilizations and a space between secular society and faith was carved out. Islam, having been born as a theocracy, is much more uneasy with the separation of church and state and the rise of secular states like Egypt, Syria, Iraq, Libya, and Turkey, and it has been met with constant resistance. It is exacerbated by the fact that Islam's geographic center is one of the economically poorest, low-performing regions of the world.

As the world has embraced liberal democracy and universal human rights, many practices found in the Islamic world such as stoning women for adultery, beheadings, cutting the hands off of thieves, honor-killings, forbidding women to have any body part showing or keeping them from driving or entering the workforce, issuing death sentences on artists, or killing homosexuals seem barbaric to the rest of the world. The modern world, many argue, has moved on from this kind of harshness.

It cannot be said that Muslims throughout history or even today are locked into a dogmatic, militant, intolerant faith. Assuredly, most Muslims throughout history have been people who just wanted to have shelter, food for their kids, and a life free of pain. These are universal desires. In many cases, they may have never met a non-Muslim. The point of this chapter is that when Islam takes on a dogmatic, militant, and intolerant form, it is easy for those militant believers to look back at Muhammad, the Quran, and centuries of Islamic imperialism and find validation of comfort with militancy—even romanticize it. Consequently, it is not that most Muslims subscribe to a faith like this, rather that violent, militant movements can loudly proclaim they are not much different than the founder, his prophetic message, and the Empire he founded. This is not the case with Christianity and other faiths.

Resistance Against Violence by Muslims and Islamic Nations

It is not true that all Islamic nations are comfortable with militant Islam. While Saudi Arabia is a *Wahhabi* nation, its government has installed cameras in mosques to monitor the messages.[21] Uzbekistan, Kazakhstan, Tajikistan, and Kuwait record messages in mosques also, and the United Arab Emirates lets very few clerics write their own sermons.[22] Turkey has a religious bureaucracy, the *Diyanet*, that monitors Islamic discourse.[23] Egypt has put extensive safeguards in place to prevent vitriolic messages from militant groups. These include requiring preachers to get government licenses and follow pre-established themes for sermons, banning talk of politics in mosques, and firing twelve thousand preachers. [24]

The fact that there is such a need to regulate Islamic preaching from clerics in so many different countries is a sign that Islam has a problem. While it is wrong to assume all Muslims are violent or condone violence, more than any other religion, Islam has large swaths of faith adherents who struggle against the core freedoms of the modern world, and this is what we are witnessing at the dawn of the twenty-first century. In Afghanistan, Jordan, and Egypt, more than 75 percent favor the death penalty for those who renounce their faith in Islam.[25] And of the top ten countries denying women their rights, nine are Muslim majority nations.[26] When a Jordanian pilot was burned alive in January 2015, shocking the whole Islamic world, the response of the much respected "moderate" Al-Azhar's Sunni Sheik in Cairo was that the appropriate punishment for such

21. "Converting the Preachers," *The Economist.* December 13, 2014. http://alturl.com/fcosz

22. Ibid.

23. Ibid.

24. Ibid.

25. http://alturl.com/m5g9q

26. Of the ten bottom-ranking countries in the World Economic Forum's report on women's rights, nine are majority Muslim countries. http://alturl.com/yio4y

a horrible sin was "killing, crucifixion, or chopping off the limbs."[27] This is clearly not the kind of punishment most liberal democracies would recommend.

While a very visible Islamic minority has chosen violence and terrorism, there are movements within Islam that are arguing for a new more peaceful way and a separation of church and state. Not all Muslims are attracted to or supportive of violence. In fact, the acts of 9/11, ISIS, the attack on the Charlie Hebdo cartoonists in Paris, the live burning of a Jordanian pilot, and other militant acts have become very embarrassing to millions of Muslims. This is creating a backlash that Westerners must recognize and applaud. For instance, the violent imposition of *Sharia* in places where ISIS has taken control are leading many in Iraq and Syria to turn toward Christianity or atheism.

The Arab Atheist Network[28] provides a forum for Arabs moving away from belief in Islam or religion of any kind. Freearabs.com[29] is an online news source that arose out of the Arab Spring and confronts "both autocrats and extremists with audacious reporting and whistle-blowing, daring opinion-writing, and creative, edgy artwork." Black Ducks on Youtube allows the airing of atheist and agnostic viewpoints.[30] "Brother Rashid" posts Youtube videos including one where he discusses how ISIS represents the rule in Islam, not the exception.[31] Journalist Brian Whitaker has written a book entitled *Arabs Without God* that interviews many Arabs about their decision to leave Islam and religious belief behind. A twitter hashtag entitled "Why we reject implementing *Sharia*," was used five thousand times

---

27. http://alturl.com/3mt3a
28. http://www.arabatheistbroadcasting.com/program/magazine
29. www.freearabs.com
30. https://www.youtube.com/channel/UCFt8pHU9jLviHacyxYfuiDw
31. https://www.youtube.com/watch?v=QxzOVSMUrGM

in twenty-four hours,[32] and *Imams* in the United Kingdom have spoken up against violence in Islam.[33] Furthermore, a number of Islamic countries have outlawed ISIS and other militant Islamic groups like ISIS.

Many Muslims are like Christians in the West; they are tired of seeing the fusion of religion and politics and prefer that their governments be completely secular. Others simply secularize as they become more educated or absorb the skeptical, modern, and postmodern thinking of the West. In the same way that evangelical Christians are not immune to the forces of secularization as churches close and youth express their doubt in church and faith, the same exact thing is happening in Muslim communities.

Unwarranted American Prejudice and Violence Against Muslims

An American Muslim is far more likely to be a victim of a terror attack than a non-Muslim American. The likelihood is not even close. This should sadden us as Christians, not make us happy. Incidents of persecution of Muslims in the United States have gone up dramatically, while the number of Americans killed by terrorists remains infinitesimally low after 9/11.

As I write this very sentence, 46-year-old Craig Stephen Hicks of Chapel Hill, North Carolina, is being arrested for shooting three Muslim university students in the head after having posted anti-Muslim comments on Facebook.[34] Muslims, mosques, and Islamic centers are regularly attacked in the United States. In one tragic case in Wisconsin, a white supremacist went into a Sikh temple and shot six people to death and wounded four, despite the fact that Sikhism is a separate religion from Islam. The same thing happened in Arizona after 9/11 when a Sikh was mistaken for a Muslim

---

32. #BBCtrending: "Why Some Arabs Are Rejecting Strict Interpretations of Sharia." http://www.bbc.com/news/blogs-trending-30181494

33. "Imams Warn British Not to Fight in Syria" Christianity Today Online July 4, 2014. http://alturl.com/k7y5c

34. http://edition.cnn.com/2015/02/11/us/chapel-hill-shooting/index.html?eref=edition

and murdered as an act of retribution. While Muslims in the United States have been attacked by fellow Americans, they themselves are helping to foil attacks on U.S. soil, but this sad irony rarely makes the news.[35]

Meanwhile, not only are Muslims in the United States overwhelmingly peaceful, they are also very prosperous and contribute greatly to American society. For instance, 63 percent of Arabs in the United States are not even Muslims, they are Christians. Because the Arab world was always filled with merchants, Muslim and Christian Arabs have been great at starting businesses in the United States and do not have hostility to the country that made their success possible. This contrasts starkly with Arabs and Muslims in Europe where the society impedes their upward mobility. A good example of this is Detroit. Many Americans are concerned about the high concentration of Arabs and Muslims in Detroit, Michigan. But the Arab-American community produces $7.7 billion annually in salaries and earnings, which is twice Detroit's annual budget.[36] The ability of Detroit to survive as a city in the next 10 years may very well depend on Middle Easterners who are willing to live in a difficult area and bring American-style entrepreneurialism to an area most Americans have abandoned.

This is often unrecognized by the rest of Americans. In Garland, Texas, in 2015, American Muslims rented a large hall to protest violence and hate in Islam. They ended up being picketed by non-Muslim Americans![37] This kind of ignorance is inexcusable. While Islam may have a long-standing problem with violence, it should be clear that there are many Muslims who can peacefully coexist in pluralistic societies and be productive and kind citizens. This is a truth we must acknowledge.

35. http://prospect.org/article/terror-plots-foiled-assistance-american-muslim-community
36. http://content.time.com/time/magazine/article/0,9171,2028057-1,00.html
37. http://alturl.com/wdfg3

Discussion Questions:

1. Do you believe all the violence in the Old Testament can be explained away?

2. Is it fair to Muslims to view historical incursions against them done by Christian Europe, Christian America, and Orthodox Russia as imperialism done in the name of Christ? Why or why not?

3. Is it realistic to think all Muslims are violent or are comfortable with violence in the name of Islam?

4. What are some key differences between the way Jesus dealt with the fallenness of this world and the way Muhammad dealt with the unholiness of this world? How did Jesus enact the "Kingdom of God," and for what purpose?

5. As a Christian do you completely reject violence (capital punishment, war, and so forth)? How would you explain your position on violence to a Muslim compared to Islam's position on violence? What are the differences? What is the same?

6. Why do you think we do not hear more about Muslims protesting violence and terrorism? Why do we not hear about how peaceful, successful, and anti-*Sharia* American Muslims are in today's America?

7. Have you ever been prejudiced against a Muslim? If so, when, where, and why?

The Terrorist Threat

In 2011, the United States somberly remembered the 10-year anniversary of the September 11 attacks on the Pentagon and World Trade Center. Clearly, the country was still suffering from post-traumatic stress after the worst attack on U.S. soil in the country's history. Our troops were still in Iraq and Afghanistan, and our news stories continued to be dominated by headlines of faraway bombings and terrorist threats.

Nevertheless, that year, the chances of an American dying in a terrorist attack were not any different than prior to September 11. The chances of a U.S. citizen dying from a terrorist in 2011 were one in 20 million.[38] One can argue that perhaps this was because we have spent $60 billion per year on the Department of Homeland Security since September 11, 2001, but even if all the thwarted attacks had been successful, the chances of an American dying in a terrorist attack were still one in 1.7 million. Compare this with the chances of dying in a car accident, which are one in 19,000, while the chances of drowning in a bathtub are one in 800,000. The chances of dying in a building fire are one in 99,000.[39]

Over-Reaction to Islamic Terrorism

The National Counterterrorism Center began tracking the deaths of private U.S. citizens in 2006. After five years, their records showed

---

38. "How Scared of Terrorism Should You Be?" in Reason.com by Ronald Bailey September 6, 2011. http://reason.com/archives/2011/09/06/how-scared-of-terrorism-should

39. Ibid.

that statistically an American was four times more likely to be struck by lightning than killed by a terrorist.[40] This included the fact that most Americans who die from a terrorist attack, die in Afghanistan or in Iraq, not on U.S. soil.[41] The National Consortium for the Study of Terrorism and Responses to Terrorism (START) found that excluding 9/11, fewer than five hundred people died in the United States from terrorist attacks (hardly any from attacks by Muslims), and the rate of attacks decreased between 2002 and 2010.[42] The chances of an Islamic terrorist killing Americans have barely changed since September 11, yet the nation has spent trillions on wars and security. Meanwhile, school shootings continue quite frequently, but most Americans seem to not be so afraid of those. It is proof that terrorism is a highly effective, low casualty way of frightening millions of people and making a point.

In 2012, START also found that the majority of terrorist attacks and fatalities had occurred in just three countries: Pakistan, Iraq, and Afghanistan. The other top targets were Nigeria, Somalia, Yemen, and Thailand, a Buddhist country where an Islamic minority routinely battles the Thai majority. In the United States, the only terror attack that occurred was the killing of six *Sikh* worshipers by a white supremacist in Oak Creek, Wisconsin.

Extremist violence in the United States between 2009 and 2015 was almost entirely done by white citizens believing in the ideology of the anti-government Patriot movement, including white supremacist groups. Ninety percent of these attacks were carried out by two people or less meaning that lower-capacity, lone-wolf terrorism by white males is our primary terrorist threat in the United States. Most

---

40. Ibid.

41. Ibid.

42. Jessica Rivinius, "Majority of Terrorist Attacks Occurred in Just a Few Countries," *National Consortium for the Study of Terrorism and Responses to Terrorism*, August 18, 2014, http://www.start.umd.edu/news/majority-2013-terrorist-attacks-occurred-just-few-countries.

Americans are not even familiar with these groups that routinely carry out terrorism in the United States, but they monitor Al-Qaeda and ISIS regularly.[43]

In 2013, a bad year for America as far as terrorism was concerned, seven U.S. civilians were killed (including contractors overseas), meaning that .07 of terror fatalities were American.[44]

That Islam is currently having a problem with terrorism cannot be denied. This will be discussed in the second half of this chapter. First the reader needs to acknowledge that the chance of being killed by an Islamic terrorist is extremely low. The junk food we eat—the chemicals, sugars, and salts even in our nice restaurants and on our vegetables—are more of a threat to us on a daily basis. So why do we constantly fear Islamic terrorism?

One reason has to do with the trauma of September 11, 2001. The United States, powerful and separated from its enemies by the world's two largest oceans, has always felt a sense of invulnerability. The fact that 19 young men armed with box cutters could bring down four planes, bring down the World Trade Center, and hit the Pentagon made Americans feel particularly vulnerable. Another reason is that our television media (particularly our news channels) focuses constantly on fear as a marketing tactic in order to stay relevant and keep their ratings up in a time when people are moving toward the Internet as their primary source for news and entertainment. Fear as a marketing tactic works because it forces the brain to stop multitasking (playing with your iPhone, surfing the web, or posting messages on Facebook) and give full attention to traditional news sources. Local news nowadays is also fear-based: child abductions, frightening storms, and criminals on the loose. Furthermore,

---

43. "Age of the Wolf," *The Southern Poverty Law Center Report*, http://www.splcenter.org/lone-wolf.

44. H.A. Goodman, "Of the 17,891 Deaths from Terrorism Last Year, 19 Were American. Let Iraqis Fight ISIS," *Huffington Post*, September 14, 2014, http://alturl.com/wv5im (accessed May 11, 2015).

television shows such as *24* or *Homeland* and movies such as *American Sniper* keep the worst and most frightening images and threats of terrorism alive in our minds.

Another less talked about aspect, however, is that human beings tend to fear threats that are less predictable and less familiar. Paul Slovick's research on Risk Perception Theory found that people are particularly afraid of unknown risks, risks that are new, and risks that can be catastrophic. Because people are used to automobile crashes and the risks that they take daily when they get into their cars, their fears are tranquilized. School shootings happen often enough that people have come to accept that it *could* happen in their child's school but believe it probably won't. But the collapse of the World Trade Center or the beheading of an American journalist introduces a new kind of event to fear, and an irrational overreaction follows.[45] Terrorists play upon those kinds of deeply held fears.

The truth is that large-scale terrorist attacks are not easy to pull off. The Al-Qaeda attacks on September 11 were unique in that the seventy or eighty people who knew of the plot were able to keep the attack a secret before it launched. (Though some evidence suggests there were warnings.) The amount of secrecy, intelligent planning, coordination, evasion of law enforcement, and just plain luck needed to pull off an attack is significant. We radically overestimate how many criminal masterminds are out there based on all the ones we see in fictional movies.

A further challenge for terrorists wanting to attack the United States or other Western countries is that the would-be terrorist is often identified and exposed by local Muslims, family members, or vigilant citizens or has been unknowingly followed by an informant.[46] This is

45. Sarah Gorman, "How Do We Perceive Risk?: Paul Slovic's Landmark Analysis," Science Blogs, http://alturl.com/w5riy

46. David Sterman, "The Myth of the Invisible Jet-Setting Jihadi," Time Magazine Online, Sept. 5, 2014, http://alturl.com/a4hw2

particularly the case in the United States where the average Muslim has assimilated very well, makes a very good living, and loves the United States. It is not as easy to be secretly militant in the United States as it might be in, say, Yemen. Americans tend to underestimate how vigilant American Muslims are about not allowing radical extremists to infiltrate their communities. This is yet another truth that does not tend to make the news very often.

Terror Pornography and How Fear Dampens Faith

Violent images have power. Many radical Muslims trace their radicalization to the day they saw the images of U.S. troops (including women, which is particularly offensive to them) pointing guns, placing dogs, and tying up captured naked Muslim men in Abu Ghraib Prison, unable to even clean themselves after going to the bathroom. The published photos caused a fury in the Islamic world. The photos preyed on the emotions, shame, and pride of Muslims.

Similarly, after two wars and poll after poll showing Americans weary of fighting and paying for wars in the Middle East, support for fighting ISIS rose dramatically as soon as ISIS started to release videos of people being beheaded. The photos preyed on the emotions and pride of Americans. Images can cause overreaction.

Al-Qaeda and ISIS have learned that there is power in an image. Filming a beheading, burning people alive in cages, or crucifying people for Western consumption works. When supporters of Bashar Assad were cutting the genitals off of children, or when barrel bombings were used indiscriminately on innocents, or when seventy times as many people were killed in Syria than were killed on 9/11, there was little debate on Western streets about what to do. Those were enormous, multiple tragedies that didn't get much publicity. But when a video circulates of a few men beheaded on a beach in Libya, worldwide panic sets in, and within days there may be a significant

military response. Violent images work for terrorist groups because we live in an extremely visual world. The greater the reaction by the West to these images, the more recruits and volunteers the terrorists get. That has been the pattern so far.

It is interesting to note, however, that many Christians in the Middle East who are truly facing persecution or even execution by Islamic militants proclaim that they are willing to forgive and want their persecutors to come to the Lord. It is as if the real life and death situation they are in forces them to look to Jesus Christ as a model of how to behave. Meanwhile in the West, where the chances of being killed by an Islamic militant are extremely low, the language of many Christians is one of fear and revenge. Could it be that we are actually so secure we don't allow the teachings of the gospel to override the cultural messages we are being bombarded with in our countries?

Jesus lived under constant threat during his three years in ministry. The people he loved and the land he loved were occupied by a foreign army. He knew the very sacred temple where he worshiped was only a few years from total destruction. People he met, traveled with, and considered friends were probably going to be persecuted, tortured, or killed by the Romans. Jesus knew his disciples would face persecution, and he knew in the garden of Gethsemane that the most ghastly form of terrorism ever committed by humanity was about to be committed: The Son of God who was completely blameless and holy would be ridiculed, tortured, and nailed to a cross where he would suffocate to death. Nevertheless, Jesus refused to be dominated by fear or the need for revenge. If anyone could be justified in demanding a violent reaction, it would be Jesus. But like many Christians in the Middle East today, Jesus' primary concern was not his suffering but salvation for all, even to the point of asking God to forgive his persecutors and, through his pain, promising paradise to a guilty thief on the cross.

Are "Islamic Terrorists" Really Islamic?

It is still taboo in many circles to suggest that terrorism is directly related to the Islamic religion. It is claimed that the terrorism of groups like ISIS and Al-Qaeda is not Islamic and not sanctioned by any religious faith. George W. Bush famously said "Islam is peace," and his successor Barack Obama has also distinguished terrorism from Islam. In general, this is good. Since the vast majority of Muslim people around the world are not involved in terrorist acts, there is no need for U.S. presidents to help terrorists recruit people by defining this as a religious war against Islam. This would be counter-productive and play into the terrorists' dualistic and sometimes apocalyptic narrative. Presidents should not fall into this trap.

The terrorist groups claim to be representing a more pure form of Islam, but they do have a habit of being very selective in their choice and interpretation of sacred texts and discard the classic methods developed by the jurists and theologians for testing the accuracy and authenticity of orally transmitted traditions.[47] It is very important for non-Muslims to understand that throughout the history of Islamic civilization, societies were rooted in law and justice to keep things in order, not wanton violence and terror.[48]

Does this mean that groups like *Al-Qaeda* and ISIS are not rooted in the Islamic faith? No. As we have seen, this is really about a deeper and more complex war *within* Islam. They may be a small minority, and they may take Islamic scriptures out of context or more literally than most Muslims, but there is no separating these ideologies from Islam. They appeal to an Islamic prophet, they reflect on moments in Islamic history, they are centered in lands that Islam has conquered, their language is the holy language of Islam (Arabic), their foundational civilization's worldview is Islamic, and they appeal to Islamic

---

47. Bernard Lewis, The *Crisis of Islam: Holy War and Unholy Terror* (New York: The Modern Library, 2003), 138.

48. Ibid., 141.

prophecies and apocalyptic visions of the future. To put it another way, their computers may be warped, unpopular, and produce bad data, but their operating systems are definitely Islamic.

Many scholars want to protest this characterization, claiming that these Islamic terrorist groups are as far removed from Islam as the snake handling Christian churches of Appalachia or the Westboro Baptist Church, which even pickets funerals of U.S. soldiers. But to continue using the computer analogy above, the standard operating system of Islam and the operating system of Islamic militants overlap in many different components.

For instance, throughout much of the Islamic world in all of its history, the punishment for leaving the Islamic faith has been death. Consequently, conversions to Christianity by Muslim people have been few and far between throughout history. This is still a very real, widespread problem throughout the Islamic world. It is not a rare occurrence. The "us versus them," mentality that terrorists promote is very much an Islamic mentality acted out by non-militant Muslim societies throughout the world. Islam is not just a religion, but also a civilization, and it is one that has transported its core values throughout the world. Genuine acceptance and integration of non-believers (not just tolerance) is not something that is inherent in the DNA of Islamic civilization. Intolerance toward non-believers, liberal democratic ideas, and even basic matters such as the value and role of women in society are widespread.

For instance, of the top ten bottom-ranking countries in the World Economic Forum's report on women's rights, nine are Muslim majority nations.[49] Or take a statistic regarding tolerance for leaving Islam: More than 75 percent of Muslims in Afghanistan, Jordan, and Egypt favor the death penalty for Muslims who renounce their faith.[50]

49. http://reports.weforum.org/global-gender-gap-report-2013/
50. http://alturl.com/epwt3

Can Islam be such a strong absolutist religion with a tradition of martyrdom, punishments for blasphemy, murder for apostasy, and declarations of *jihad* and not have those ideas hijacked by terrorists and taken to their greatest extremes? As we have seen in this short book, there is enough of a history of violence and territorial expansion done throughout the very foundation of Islam's scripture and through the life of the prophet to suggest that the faith is comfortable with violence to a degree other faiths are not. A late political scientist referred to "Islam's bloody borders," in his book *The Clash of Civilizations*, but the overwhelming amount of terrorism in warfare in the world today revolves around societies that are part of the Islamic world.[51] The fact that many nations where Islam is dominant do not conform to ideas of liberal democracy or "universal human rights," suggests that Islam is, at the very least, having a hard time defining how peaceful it really is.

In other words, the story of Muhammad, the verses in the *Quran*, and the numerous *Hadith* give terrorism ample Islamic language and Islamic theological ideas and concepts to justify violence. Terrorism and violence may be a deviation of what most Muslims of the world believe, but it is clearly a part of the Islamic operating system (religion and civilization). That is why, as we saw previously, even in Islamic nations throughout the world, mosques, *Imams*, and sermons are often censored or monitored. Clearly, the language, history, and ideas of Islam can easily be interpreted in a way that many peaceful Muslims, Islamic governments, and citizens of the world find uncomfortable to say the least.

In the most recent Freedom House report on democracy and freedom around the world, ratings for the Middle East, North Africa, and Central Asia scored lower than any other part of the world. The

---

51. Samuel P. Huntington. The Clash of Civilizations and the Remaking of the World Order. New York: Touchstone, 1997. Pp. 254-258.

lack of freedom in politics in the majority of the Islamic world is inevitably linked to the lack of free thought allowed in the Islamic worldview that dominates it. The debate over *Sharia* in Islamic communities and the widespread praise of *Sharia* by various terrorist groups throughout the world are other examples of how terrorists appeal to Islamic traditions and the limitations of non-Islamic definitions of freedom.

We have also seen how Muslim tradition divides the world into two houses: The House of Islam (*Dar al-Islam*), in which Muslim law rules, and the House of War (*Dar al-Harb*), the rest of the world, which is not only made up of infidels, but is ruled by them as well. This is another example of a deep, Islamic idea the terrorists draw from. From Muhammad's farewell address in 632 CE, to Saladin five hundred years later, to the *Ayatollah* Khomeini in 1979, to Osama bin Laden in 2001, the language and commitment to "fight all men until they say 'there is no god but Allah,'" has been a constant refrain from Islamic leaders throughout Islamic history, because unlike in Christianity, this temporal world is to be conquered.

Many Muslims do subscribe to global ideas of tolerance, the value of diversity, the value of women, and the need for freedom of speech, separation of church and state, and human rights. But are these things indisputably insisted upon at all times by the revelation found in the *Quran* and the *Hadith*? No, the *Quran* is not very conducive to liberal values. Instead, it is even possible to find the sanctioning of beheading in the *Quran*.[52]

Without the clarity of a peaceful prophet like Jesus, (who was himself tortured but preached turning the other cheek), nor a separation between "the things of Caesar and God," there is a lack of agreement about who has authority and too many voices of genuine negative influence in Islam. From the *Ayatollah* in Iran, to

52. http://www.meforum.org/713/beheading-in-the-name-of-islam

the Saudi cleric Muhammad Al-Arefe (who has more followers on Twitter than the Pope), to voices of extremist Imams in places like London and Paris, Islam is an absolutist faith that has a tremendous prophetic leadership vacuum that empowers the most violent and radical spokespersons.

Islam has been unable to carve out a public space in which to openly and safely debate its core identity once and for all. Islam has not had its reformation nor been able to get beyond its "Christendom" moment. Even the large divide between *Sunni* and *Shia* seems to be one where violence, murder, and genocide are viewed with understanding. We would find it odd today if Roman Catholics, Protestants, and Eastern Orthodox Christians were arguing for the total physical decimation through physical violence of another branch of the Christian faith, would we not?

There are reformers out there such as Majiid Nawaz, but they are not usually well-known. Just as there has been no Islamic peaceful Messiah, there have been no Islamic Martin Luthers, Martin Luther King Jrs, or Gandhis. There have been no great figures in Islam who have redefined the faith's view on how its absolutist nature can be enacted in a way that completely steers clear of violence or can be in harmony with the rest of the world's civilizations and religions. Furthermore, many Islamic nations (and the territorial heart of Islam, Arabia) are shame-based cultures where honor must be protected at all costs, and for many Muslims, the decline of Islamic civilization is a thing of shame that must be avenged eventually. That is very much in line with the ideas of the *Quran*. Compare this with the Bible, which ends with a book (Revelation) about a persecuted church.

Christianity, while it started in the Middle East, had many of its most militant and ethnocentric tendencies tempered by Jesus, by Roman law, by democracy, and by secular humanism (which it gave birth to). The absence of a process such as this is what leads to ideas that infidels must not be allowed to practice their faith in Saudi Arabia, that the writer Salman Rushdie should die because of blasphemy in a work of fiction, or that it is necessary to kill a relative who has dishonored the family by becoming a Christian.

While this book has argued that there are hundreds of millions of peaceful Muslims as well as entire countries that are really quite secular or where Christians can live next to Muslims with no problems, Islam has a historical, cultural, and civilizational heritage that terrorists constantly appeal to in their acts of violence—beginning with their respect for Muhammad and their reading of the *Quran*. This fact seems inescapable.

Discussion Questions

1. How worried are you about being killed in a terrorist attack? Do you think your level of worry is in proportion to reality?

2. What are some of the reasons that we fear low-risk events more than high-risk events? What in our culture might fuel an overreaction to terrorism?

3. What is Scripture's overall view on how we are to think about death? Does this factor into our thinking when we are afraid of terrorism?

4. What types of reforms are needed in the Islamic world? Do you see some taking place? Why are others not taking place?

5. Despite the reluctance of many, why does the author say that it is fair game to label Islamic terrorists as Islamic? What are some of the many reasons the author gives for how this is rooted in the Islamic faith? Do you agree or disagree?

The Future of the Islamic World

W hat does the future of the Islamic world hold? Will the Arab Spring ultimately lead to a wave of democratization as happened in Eastern Europe? Or will groups like *Al-Qaeda*, ISIS, and *Boko Haram* continue to rise up and seize control of the Islamic world? Will terrorism be contained or will it spread deeper and farther into the West, Africa, Asia, and Latin America? In this chapter, we will look at how the Islamic world arrived at this moment of disarray and what this means for the coming decades.

A New World Disorder

After the end of the Cold War (1945–1991), we entered into a period of rapid communication, political change, economic integration, and global interdependency. The term "globalization" was used to describe this moment, but since globalization is always occurring to some extent, I use the term *hyper*-globalization to describe an unusually rapid time of global integration. With the collapse of the Soviet Union, Communism seemed to have been disproven as a viable political and economic system, and capitalism and democracy appeared to have won the day. The number of democracies grew at a dramatic pace in the 1990s and the vast majority of the world sought to integrate into the Western, free-market style of economics.

Globalization raised the overall living standards of the world at a dramatic speed. Twenty years after the fall of the Berlin Wall, the number of people living in absolute poverty around the world had decreased to less than a billion, better *by far* than at any time in human history. A new global middle class emerged throughout the world, most notably in the poor countries of China and India that transitioned from being places of widespread, extreme poverty to having a middle class as large as the entire population of the United States. China has more than three hundred million in its emerging middle class, and the average person in India is now wealthier than the average Russian!

But globalization, democracy, and the new Post-Cold War era also created a large gap between the rich and poor in most countries. While many underdeveloped countries were seeing an emerging middle class, in previously economically developed countries (Japan, the United States, the United Kingdom), the middle class was shrinking as both the wealthy class and the underclass grew. Globalization raises human living standards overall, but it also creates a large gap between rich and poor.

In the Islamic world, the end of the Cold War meant that Marxism was no longer a realistic ideology to create an effective political and economic system. Unfortunately, neither was true democracy as most of these countries were either under the hand of strong-armed oppressive rulers, had no history of democracy, or were filled with tribal ethnic groups that had only been living peacefully with each other because they were forced to by their oppressive governments. With a lack of ideologies to order society, militant Islam became a new ideology to challenge Middle Eastern, North African, Russian, Central Asian, and Western oppressors. The belief that took hold was that if one could restore classic Islamic society, all would be right with the world. Islamic Fascism filled an ideological gap now that Arab nationalism, authoritarianism, and Marxism had been discredited.

The decision to invade Iraq and overthrow Saddam Hussein created a new leadership vacuum in the most volatile part of the world, ancient Mesopotamia. While Saddam was a ruthless leader, Iraq served as a balance against Iran and Syria, kept tribal violence under control, and made it difficult for terrorist groups like ISIS and *Al-Qaeda* to inhabit this dangerous region. With the collapse of the Hussein regime, all of these problems returned with a vengeance, and Iraq became a safe haven for terrorists, ethnic militias, and for outside powers to manipulate in many directions. It is now a hotbed of militancy and terrorism.

Religious militancy and terrorism have always been a way to rally people against unfair governments, economic systems, or land disputes. This does not occur only within Islam. The Tamil Tigers in Sri Lanka did a similar thing in the name of Hinduism. However, because Muhammad called his followers to create an Islamic world on this Earth, Islam can be particularly easy to turn into a religious-political ideology, and that is what *Al-Qaeda*, ISIS, *Boko Haram*, and many other groups have done.

As I argued in my 2006 book *Passport of Faith: A Christian's Encounter with World Religions,* periods of *hyper*-globalization always create a counteraction in which new ideologies will arise to challenge the world order.[53] Islamic militancy has all the ingredients to serve as the primary mode of resistance to globalization in the Islamic world for many years to come. Trying to usher in a "fair and just" Islamic world under the "blessing of God" that takes everyone back to a "golden period" is a powerful message for people who are feeling oppressed and left behind in this new world order. In societies with low literacy rates, large populations of youth, great poverty, and traditional values, this is a particularly appealing message.

---

53. Patrick Nachtigall, *Passport to Faith: A Christian's Encounter with World Religions* (Anderson: Warner Press, 2006).

The Impossible Vortex of the Middle East

The coming collapse of Yemen is an example of what is happening to the Middle East as a whole. *Sunni* Saudi Arabia and *Shia* Iran are funding militias in that country, and in the absence of a strong central government, the government is collapsing, leaving a failed state that is rife with violence and terrorism.[54] This has also happened in Syria and Iraq. Within countries like Yemen, there are U.S. backed and *Al-Qaeda* backed militias. The loss of authority in the Middle East has created a vacuum for terrorist groups to operate. Terrorist groups can then also exploit the *Sunni-Shia* divide, thus further dividing the Middle East, expanding the reach of terrorism, and pulling the West into further confrontation. It is a vicious cycle that will continue for the foreseeable future.

In the same way the United States and the Soviet Union fought proxy wars away from their homelands in places like Central America and Southeast Asia, today *Sunni* and *Shia* nations are starting their own proxy wars by sponsoring militias in the Middle East and North Africa. The American response is to find militias within that morass to sponsor. These are then labeled "moderate groups." The support of moderate groups is inevitably encouraging sectarianism that wasn't present before. The moderate groups are then just as prone to vendettas and bloodletting as the original terrorist groups.

In other words, large Arab states are sponsoring *Shia* and *Sunni* militias and governments to gain influence in the region and thwart each other. The United States is funding militias to stop terrorism. These civil wars disintegrate countries and create ethnic and religious tribalism. Terrorist groups like ISIS and *Al-Qaeda* exploit the breakdown of countries like Libya, Syria, Iraq, and Yemen and even join

---

54. On the day this chapter was finished, Saudi Arabia began bombing Yemen with a coalition of Arab states, the leader of Yemen had been overthrown, and the U.S. was pulling back its presence in the country. The collapse seems to have begun as Sunni and Shia faceoff to see who will control Yemen and its territory, which makes for a perfect host for terrorist groups.

up forces occasionally with other militias. In return, the U.S. and the West sponsor militias that foster further divisions and desires for revenge.

Sometimes the divide is between *Sunni* and *Shia*, other times it is between separatists and nationalists, and still other times it is between democrats and authoritarians. Inevitably, it all gets mixed together and ends up also being about criminal networks, access to resources, age-old tribal feuds, or the opportunity to make millions of dollars from countries like the United States, Saudi Arabia, and Iran. No side ends up fighting fairly and all sides, from ISIS to the "freedom fighters," end up with a culture of violence, torture, and corruption. True peaceful reformers are swallowed up by the vortex created by the collapse of order in the Middle East, and all of this is set within an Islamic culture that has not been able to absorb enough liberal democratic ideas in its key institutions.

This leads to strange situations such as when America's traditional enemy Iran is using its *Shia* forces to attack *Sunni* ISIS terrorists in Iraq, but those same forces are also propping up the regime in Syria, which we also detest. It is even more odd that ISIS fights the Iranians and U.S forces with U.S. military equipment that American-backed militias either lost in previous fights or left behind, or even worse, because the former U.S. allies joined sides with ISIS.

The United States and Western nations get caught in another trap. If they join sides with their enemies (like Iran) to fight another enemy (like ISIS) and win a battle, they will be held responsible for all the violent revenge bloodletting that will follow. If they do not get involved, the war against the terrorist groups ends up being lost or led by our enemies. It is truly a no-win situation. To further compound the difficulty, in many cases the Middle East conspiracy theory belief is that ISIS is just a creation of the United States and

Israel anyway—a way of further gaining control of the Middle East. The vortex inevitably wins, not law and order.

Why People Will Continue to Choose to Join Terrorist Groups

Terrorism provides a source of funding and material wealth. ISIS sells oil, steals valuable museum pieces to sell on the black market (when not destroying them), and robs banks. The Taliban taxes opium and raisins; *Al Qaeda* uses Muslim non-profit organizations and charities to dabble in drug sales, raise money for individuals, and to pay for terrorist activities. In the poorly governed African states of Chad, Cameroon, Nigeria, and Niger, *Boko Haram* (which means "Western education is sacrilege") kidnaps women, missionaries, and children to demand ransom payments. Sex-trafficking will continue to be another way that terrorist groups can fund their activities; some might even make that their primary business. Access to women for sex is yet another primary motivation for many terrorists who come from societies where the mingling of the sexes is greatly discouraged. Testosterone and the adrenaline rush of a great adventure are also key motivators for many young men to join terrorist groups. Never underestimate the power of testosterone. Young males in their prime are far more likely to join terrorist groups and commit crimes. Terrorism is about much more than "the cause" or some spiritual *jihad*; it is often about economics, greed, sex, and the globalization of criminal networks, which are then spiritualized using the language and symbols of Islamic history.

In terrorist groups, inevitably, there are genuine believers who are waging a violent *jihad* in the name of Islam. Others are genuine psychopaths committed to totally annihilating their enemies. Many of the top leaders and executioners fall into this category. Others are impressionable youth or naïve people looking for adventure who fall for the simplistic theology and ideology of the terrorist groups. They may have been targeted by terrorist recruiters who know how to look for broken, vulnerable, and impressionable youth in order to give them a new purpose for life and a new "family" to belong to.

Many young terrorists have romantic dreams of what the terrorist group may offer: glory, money, sex with a woman for the first time, martyrdom, or an escape from their dreary lives. These young men rarely know anything about Islam. In some cases, they come from countries where there are no opportunities and they have little education, so they are recruited into a "holy war," or they are disgruntled youth from Western countries. Some may be veterans of other Islamic militant wars in places like Chechnya and Afghanistan who are committed to join other global causes for "Islamic justice."

Still another group would be those who live in failed states or with corrupt governments that do not provide for their people. They may find that the terrorist group (*Hamas*, *Hezbollah*, *Al-Qaeda*, ISIS, and so on) provides social services, food, or money when their own government cannot. It is these terrorist organizations that bring bread and education to their children. Still others may be forced to join the terrorist organization at gunpoint or be killed or have their entire families killed. They are hostages who are forced to become terrorists. It is tragic to think of those who have been forced into the terrorist lifestyle by force—especially children—but it happens frequently. Many children and youth are kidnapped and systematically trained and forced to become killers through a process of desensitization. The damage they do to the psyche is severe and the process of healing for those who escape is a very difficult one.

Finally others join terrorist organizations to create an alliance against another army (as happened in Syria when "Freedom Fighters" joined *Al-Qaeda* to fight Bashar Assad's oppressive regime). As we can see, believing that all Islamic terrorists joined Islamic terrorism because they were truly committed to Islam is a fallacy. In many cases, many Islamic militants know very little about the *Quran* and Islamic theology. They can be pulled in by a variety of factors that do not have anything to do with Islam.

Future Fault Lines in the Islamic World

The Middle East

The disintegration of governments and law and order in parts of the Islamic world will lead to new militant insurgencies and terrorist activity. While the rise of Islamic militancy will continue to push Islam toward some reform and accommodation with aspects of liberal democratic values, many Muslims will continue to be disillusioned and turn toward Christianity, secularism, or other faiths. Fundamentalist regimes and Islamic militants will continue to be viewed as being incapable of creating an innovative, modern society. This process of discrediting militant Islam could take years or decades. Technically, it could take centuries.

The cycle of violence that we see in Yemen and throughout Mesopotamia will continue for the foreseeable future. The borderlines are shifting, the countries involved are getting poorer, infrastructure is being destroyed, and ethnic feuds and rivalries are being aggravated to such a degree that the cycle will not be stopped by any outside force.

The *Alawites, Kurds, Druze, Shia, Sunni,* and non-Muslim groups like the *Yazidis, Manicheans, Mandaeans,* and Christians, as well as other ancient religions will continue to clash and some of these smaller, less-known minority religions will be in danger of being extinguished completely.

Nations like Turkey, Egypt, Tunisia, and Iran that have strong, ancient national identities will remain intact and could possibly flourish economically, but will inevitably face insurgencies. Nations like Libya, Yemen, Iraq, and Syria that had very weak national identities to begin with will cease to have functioning governments and become anarchical and tribal. They will be hosts for terrorist groups and criminal networks.

In some ways, the rise of *Al-Qaeda* has been a bit of a blessing to Israel. The world, particularly Arab states, is not that concerned about Palestinians anymore. There is no longer much blaming of Israel for the troubles of the region, because the focus is on authoritarian rulers, corrupt Islamic regimes, and dangerous militant groups threatening entire nations. The civil war within Islam is distracting people from the Israel-Palestine situation.

Israel, however, finds itself in a more unstable and unpredictable neighborhood than before. Its failure to offer a two-state solution, take care of the humanitarian crisis in Gaza, and refusal to stop settlements has eroded its support not only in Europe; but even among Jewish Americans. There has been little effort to stabilize the country, and as a democracy with a large population of Arabs (Christian and Muslim), Israel now faces the possibility that it will become an apartheid state that is openly segregationist the way South Africa and the United States once were. This would bring global condemnation and make it hard for even the United States to continue supporting it. It will be a race to see whether Israel will give up on democracy or become embroiled in a Middle Eastern war first. Hopefully, it will be neither. But the collapse of Syria has decreased Israel's security. A collapse of Lebanon or Jordan as well as increasing militancy in the Sinai Peninsula will be a huge security problem.

It is important to remember that as much as the Middle Eastern countries hate Israel, they often cooperate with Israel behind the scenes because these countries also fear Islamic militancy. Furthermore, with between two hundred and four hundred nuclear weapons, the best military in the region, and an alliance with the United States, the nations of the Middle East (including Iran) are far more afraid of Israel's power than they are willing to let on in their rhetoric. A loss in a war to a Jewish state would be humiliating and guarantee the end of any regime that waged that war. It would be total humiliation for the leader and generals.

Some Islamic militants, however, would have no such fear and believe the more apocalyptic and violent the battle, the better. But it is precisely this nihilistic attitude that will make unity within terrorist groups hard to achieve for big, significant battles.

Africa

Africa will become the next major front in the civil war that is happening within Islam. Over the past ten years, the United States has quietly been establishing military bases throughout Africa to deal with the eventual rise of terrorism and Islamic militancy in Africa. *Boko Haram* is the first African terrorist organization to really become a household name, but there will be others. Many North African countries are landlocked, mostly desert-filled with differing tribes, and economically backward. They will have all the ingredients to support Islamic militancy and create chaos.

North Africa is primarily Muslim. Everything south of the Sahara desert is Christian. There are 1.1 billion Africans, and it is estimated that by 2025 there will be 633 million Christians in Africa.[55] In the competition between Islam and Christianity for converts on African soil, the Christians are winning overwhelmingly. This is going to cause further tensions as we have seen in the African countries of Nigeria and the Sudan (now divided into two countries; the Islamic North and the Christian South). Many of the ingredients that fuel terrorism and anarchy in the Middle East will be present in North and Central Africa. African countries with more moderate Muslim populations and located far south of the equatorial fault line, will

---

55. World Council of Churches Report, August 2004.

have the opportunity to develop economically further than they ever have in their history. Meanwhile, Christianity will continue to out-grow Islam in Africa.

Russia

The country in the world that receives the most immigrants each year is not the United States, but Russia. Many of these immigrants come from Central Asian countries that were formerly Soviet satel-lites and have an Islamic heritage. With a rapidly aging workforce, the workers are needed to keep the Russian economy moving. However, Russia's relationship with its Islamic former Soviet Republics is not all smooth. The two horrific wars for independence from Russia in Chechnya are an example of how ancient hostilities against Russia can be renewed and lead toward a new Islamic militancy. Many of the Chechen fighters had never read a *Quran* or practiced Islam until the war broke out. But as we have mentioned, religion is often infused to create a more cohesive identity and purpose. Russia in the future may easily find itself surrounded by Islamic militants. There have been a number of terrorist attacks in Russia done by Islamic militants including the horrific murder of school children in Beslan in 2004 and a string of suicide bombers in Moscow. Unlike the United States, Russia is truly surrounded by countries that are breeding grounds for terrorists who can easily cross their borders. The United States is far more protected from Islamic militancy than Russia or Europe, yet it tends to panic more about it than any other country in the world. This is not logical or helpful.

Europe

The threat of an Islamic invasion in Europe is vastly over-drama-tized in the media. Usually the dire predictions are based on the high birthrate of Muslims in Europe. But straight-line projections are erroneous. Sometimes the predictions are based on the fact that there are neighborhoods in cities like Amsterdam or Paris where Muslim communities practice *Sharia* and view that as a higher authority than the law of the country.

But there are a few realities that are often not mentioned. National police forces and Interpol in Europe are extremely good at monitoring terrorist activity. Europe's decision to invest in policing rather than military interventions as the United States did, has been far more effective at creating security with far less expense.

Neither is Europe in danger of being outnumbered by Muslims. Most Western European nations have an Islamic population between 2 and 6 percent. Only France has an unusually high population of Muslims at 10 percent. Birthrates are coming in line with the rest of Europe, and most Muslims simply want to become financially prosperous and give their children a good life.

Most likely, immigration to European countries for Muslims will get much more difficult in the future. Furthermore, there will most likely be a movement to reign in the freedom of new immigrants and there will be stiffer requirements for assimilation. Right-wing parties have been calling for this in Europe, but in alarmist and racist fashion. Probably, Europe will choose a path between being reactionary and gently raising its expectations of Islamic citizens, while continuing to believe that pluralistic societies are vital to Europe's security—which is true. Underneath Europe's mask of tolerance lie ancient well-known fault lines and tensions that are never fully erased. Europe's challenge will be to deal with increasing economic pressures, immigration, and racial pressures in a way that won't inflame the situation. Europe is highly unlikely to be involved in large-scale war against Islamic countries, as it would serve virtually no purpose for them economically or strategically. Europe will continue to be at odds with the way the United States deals with the challenge of Islamic militancy with its more aggressive, yet geographically distant approach.

The chaos the U.S. creates in the Middle East more directly affects Europe than the United States—through refugee crises for instance.

Furthermore, Muslims, like Christians, are often very influenced by the culture, education, and society around them and become quite secular. Most Muslims simply want to become financially prosperous and give their children a good life. While many Muslim youth feel disenfranchised from full integration in European countries, most will turn to the things most frustrated global youth turn to (drugs, sex, video games, gangs, rap music, and so forth), not militant Islam. Of course, those who do will make the headlines and there will inevitably be attacks on key locations in Europe over the coming years. But Europeans, unlike Americans, have never lived under the illusion that terrorism can be fully eradicated. Having dealt with terrorist groups and waves of terrorist attacks in Northern Ireland, the United Kingdom, Germany, Spain, France, and other places throughout the past thirty years, the European attitude has a more realistic view about terrorism: It cannot be fully eradicated and it is a nuisance more than it is an existential threat. Europe's primary concern with terrorism (unlike the United States) is the attack on civil discourse and pluralism that Europe has worked so hard to create in the aftermath of World War II. The threat to open societies is Europe's greatest fear, not total destruction. Terrorism can never be completely eradicated in any society.

The U.S.A.

Recent attacks in Sydney, Ottawa, Paris, and other global cities have shown that "the West" is still a target for Islamic militants. In rhetoric, the United States is always a popular target. But with Canada and Mexico as neighbors and the world's two largest oceans on its east and west, the United States is far safer from Islamic militancy than China, Russia, the countries of Africa and the Middle

East, Israel, and most other nations in the world. Yet it is the country that has most been obsessed with the terrorist attacks.

Much of this is due to the trauma of having been attacked on U.S. soil for the first time on September 11, 2001. Ten years later, the United States had spent five trillion dollars on the War on Terror.[56] That figure continues to grow despite the fact that other countries have been able to police terror just as well as the United States for a fraction of the cost. Furthermore, the bulk of terrorist attacks occur in Pakistan, Iraq, Syria, and other nations ensconced within the Islamic world and far away from U.S. shores.

The United States, as we saw in Chapter 6, has traditionally had Middle Easterners who are Christians immigrate to the country. Many Orthodox, Catholic, and Protestant Middle Easterners chose to settle in the United States and don't pose a threat. Most Muslims in the United States come from the upper classes and are economically successful and wealthy—doing even better financially than the average American. Unlike in Europe, Muslims in the United States have not had upward mobility denied to them. The United States is far better at making new immigrants feel like U.S. citizens than European countries, because citizenship is based on an idea, not on ethnicity. American Muslims may have very conservative views such as believing the *Quran* to be without flaws (even though they have vastly different interpretations). They also have very conservative social mores, and believe that God comes above country. But many evangelicals feel the exact same way.[57] As Christians, we don't find this threatening, but logical. When the shoe is on the other foot, however, we find it strange and unpatriotic.

It is hard not to believe that the United States overreacted to the terrorist threat after 9/11. As discussed in Chapter 6, terrorism

---

56. http://nation.time.com/2011/06/29/the-5-trillion-war-on-terror/
57. http://alturl.com/55px2

is simply not that good at conquering territory, ushering in new empires, or being able to hurt large numbers of people over and over again. It does, however, carry powerful symbolism and does terrorize people's psyches causing the people to inflate the danger level. The United States trained its people to live under constant alerts and to invest in a military response, instead of the European approach of better policing and expecting calm from the citizens. Since terrorism is not an existential threat to the United States, the country will have to turn a corner (as it started to after the Boston Marathon Bombing in 2013) and begin to practice a business-as-usual approach to terrorist attacks. The attack in Boston was shocking and shut down the whole city, yet it barely made the news 10 days later. This was a good sign and a positive step in the right direction. This will have to be the norm in the future because the United States cannot live in a perpetual state of irrational fear of something that has only a one in twenty million chance of killing an American.

The United States, however, will be very tempted to remain militarily engaged all over the world. The first reason is that while the U.S. is no longer truly dependent on Middle Eastern oil (Saudi Arabia is only our sixth largest exporter now), the nation's economy is dependent on East Asia's economies, which are absolutely in need of Middle Eastern oil. Keeping shipping lanes open in the Persian Gulf and the Indian Ocean will continue to be a top priority for the U.S.

A second pressure will be that as terror networks spread, only the United States military will have the ability to strike globally. The question will be whether the United States will get trapped in land wars it cannot win, or whether it will focus on strategic strikes. It will also need to learn not to create new vacuums for terrorists as it did in Iraq and Libya.

A third formidable pressure will be the military industrial complex, which is deeply influential in both the Democrat and Republican parties. The pressure will continue to mount on U.S. presidents to show that they are "tough on terror" by using military might. Americans are still very likely to punish any president who is viewed as weak for not using military force. By and large, Americans trust military force even when it doesn't work.

The greatest military challenge to the United States when fighting terrorists and countries that harbor terrorism is that they will find themselves fighting a pre-modern enemy, in a modern war, in a postmodern world. What does this mean? It means that Islamic militants will be only too happy to hide behind mosques, hospitals, women, and children, and bait the United States into land wars. Islamic militants follow a pre-modern code of conduct that makes even innocents fair game. The only way to fight them is to take their territory away (as in modern warfare), but this will involve killing innocents. For the rest of the world, which has a postmodern skepticism about violence and a strong belief in protecting all innocents, the sight of U.S. troops striking hospitals, women, children, or other innocents will cause anger and a loss of confidence in the U.S. This trap was clearly visible in the Iraq War and it will be more difficult in the future if we are fighting nihilistic or apocalyptic terrorist groups.

The United States will continue to find itself trapped. It will never be able to pacify the Middle East because it is not willing to do what it would take: colonize the Middle East, as previous empires did. Colonization would involve far more than military troops and bombing. It would require U.S. citizens in large numbers moving to the troubled spots of the world and creating American-based institutions, running them, and teaching others how to run them as the British and Romans did. Since Americans have no interest in that kind of colonization (nor is it that acceptable in the modern world), there will be an inability to gain control of the situation. The civil war within Islam will have to play itself out. Thus the United States will need to learn to avoid full-on wars with a pre-modern enemy and instead invest in education, institutions, youth programs, and militarily to find a way to serve as a global strike force against terrorism with a much smaller footprint.

Central Asia

Central Asia's authoritarian, weak, and poor nations will see their futures depend on their relationship with power-players like Iran and Russia. The more they enter into Russia's sphere of influence, the less well they will do economically. Russia will need to continue an attempt to create an economic union that will be their version of the European Union or NAFTA to create economic opportunities and serve as an alternative to Western economic alliances, in addition to regaining control over their former Soviet-Satellites.

Russia is surrounded by countries with high Islamic populations, and they have already seen how militants in Chechnya became immersed in Islam, which led to two incredibly destructive wars between Chechnya and Russia. There have also been numerous attacks on Russia by Islamic militants (including the 1999 apartment building bombings that seem to have been an inside job by Russian security services in order to blame the Chechens and consolidate Putin's power). Central Asia has not been in the news much, but it may be in the future if Central Asia becomes as unsettled as the Middle East.

Iran will most likely emerge out of the doldrums after years of watching its Islamic Revolution fail on every level imaginable. It has the opportunity to return to being a key power in the region economically as well as militarily. Adjusting to a rising Iran will be difficult for the Middle East, which is used to the *Shia* state being more reigned-in and economically stagnant. Iran's emergence will lead to a more open Cold War with Saudi Arabia and other key *Sunni* States, or it will lead to proxy wars and economic war in, which Iran forces the other nations to compete more than they have for influence and control of the region.

Westerners often think that Iran's great enemies are Israel and the United States. This is because they take Iranian rhetoric at face value. But in reality, Iran's primary enemy is Saudi Arabia. The two countries are divided religiously (the Saudis are *Sunni* and the Iranians are *Shia*); both want to dominate the world oil market, and both fund terrorist groups but for different branches of the Islamic faith. Saudi Arabia has the superior air force, but Iran has an arsenal of missiles that could destroy Saudi Arabian cities. Iran can also practice cyber-warfare, shut the straits of Hormuz in the Persian Gulf where the oil flows, and mobilize groups like *Hezbollah* and other groups in Yemen.

Overall, Saudi Arabia is a declining power, while Iran has the opportunity to become a rising power. This will create great tension, especially as Turkey is also a rising power on the *Sunni* side. The civil war within Islam may primarily be held and financed by these two enemies.

South Asia and Southeast Asia

Southeast Asia will have its fortunes mainly dictated by the rise or decline of China and India. Conflicts that involve Islam in this region will be less volatile and expansive than in the Middle East and Africa and more about local ethnic battles such as the ones that occur in Thailand and the Philippines. The one country that promises to continue as a source of global instability and a source of terrorism and militant Islam will be Pakistan which will remain ungovernable and will treat Afghanistan as its vassal state. Its primary conflict though, will continue to be against its traditional enemy, India. India, a primarily Hindu nation that also has the second largest population of Muslims in the world, will continue to outperform Pakistan economically and maintain its rivalry with China.

On the micro-level, it will continue to be very difficult to be a Christian in many of these countries, particularly Pakistan, India, and Bangladesh. The Christian church may be in a lot of conflict with Islam even though the countries themselves may not be caught up in the bigger Islamic civil war. Christians will need to monitor Christian persecution in South Asia and Southeast Asia closely, because it will not be in the news as much as events in the Middle East and Africa. It will also come from Buddhist and Hindu groups opposed to the gospel, not just Islamic groups.

Fear Is the Enemy of Mission

Regardless of what happens in the future, Christians around the world must avoid giving in to a spirit of constant fear, and instead trust in the fact that God is continuing to make himself known around the world. Our call as followers of Christ is not to live in the safest world possible or to get into a self-protective fear-based posture. Our call is to be the salt of the earth and go and make disciples of all nations, baptizing them in the name of the Father and of the Son and of the Holy Spirit. We must condemn the spirit of fear that easily engulfs Western Christians regarding Islam. This crisis in the Islamic world is an opportunity. Fear, on the other hand, is the enemy of mission.

We have already seen how, for the vast majority of Western Christians (particularly Americans), Islamic terrorism is not an existential threat and in fact is not even very dangerous at all on a daily basis. The greater danger is for us to give in to hatred, prejudice, or paralyzing fear instead of a genuine concern for the souls and safety of Muslims, Christian missionaries on the front lines, and Christian communities truly facing persecution and extinction.

Being countercultural as Jesus was, will involve rejecting fear and panic, mobilizing behind missionaries in the Islamic world, caring for and welcoming refugees who come to our shores, seeking friendship with those whose belief systems are radically different than ours, and praying for Muslims to see Jesus, instead of wishing them harm and destruction.

In Romans 14:11, Paul, who was himself martyred, reminds us that "every knee will bow and every tongue will confess." We know how the grand story of humankind will end: with Jesus Christ ushering in his kingdom in its fullness. Until then, our command is to love God with all of our heart and with all of our soul and with all of our mind; and to love our neighbor as ourselves (Matthew 22:37).

During this turbulent time for the Islamic world, we will continue to see civil wars, beheadings, and acts of terrorism in public places. If the strong images coming out of the Islamic world in crisis are powerful in their terror, let us make sure that the images coming out of the Christian church are the exact opposite.

Discussion Questions

1. What are some of the reasons people join terrorist groups? How many of these reasons have to do with fervent religious belief? Do any of these reasons surprise you?

2. What is your response to youth who are captured by militants or told that their whole family will be killed if they do not join a terrorist group? How would you respond in that situation?

3. Which of the regions discussed seems the most volatile? Why?

4. What are some of the traps that the author says the U.S. and other Western nations are caught in as they try to fight militant Islam?

5. Why does the author suggest other countries have less confidence in military force than the U.S. does in dealing with the problem of terrorism?

6. How does our society encourage us to respond with fear and panic regarding terrorism?

7. What are some ways you or your church can break the mold and respond to the challenges of the Islamic world in a Christ-like manner?

CPSIA information can be obtained at www.ICGtesting.com
Printed in the USA
LVOW01s0405210515

439206LV00003B/3/P